MAVERICK REAL ESTATE FINANCING

MAVERICK REAL ESTATE FINANCING

The Art of Raising Capital
and Owning Properties
Like Ross, Sanders, and Carey

STEVE BERGSMAN

WILEY

John Wiley & Sons, Inc.

Published by John Wiley & Sons, Inc., Hoboken, New Jersey
Published simultaneously in Canada

For general information on our other products and services or for technical support, please contact our Customer Care Department within the United States at (800) 762-2974, outside the United States at (317) 572-3993 or fax (317) 572-4002.

Wiley also publishes its books in a variety of electronic formats. Some content that appears in print may not be available in electronic books. For more information about Wiley products, visit our web site at www.wiley.com.

Library of Congress Cataloging-in-Publication Data
Bergsman, Steve.
    Maverick real estate financing : the art of raising capital and owning properties like Ross, Sanders, and Carey / Steve Bergsman.
        p. cm.
    Includes bibliographical references.
    ISBN-13: 978-0-471-74587-7 (cloth)
    ISBN-10: 0-471-74587-1 (cloth)
    1. Real estate investment. 2. Real property—Finance. I. Title.
    HD1382.5.B467 2006
    332.63'24—dc22
                                                                        2005029364

Printed in the United States of America
10 9 8 7 6 5 4 3 2 1

To my lovely wife, Wendy,
and my two, wonderful boys,
Ethan and Aaron

Contents

Introduction

The inspiration for *Maverick Real Estate Financing* derived from my experiences promoting my first book, *Maverick Real Estate Investing.*

When I undertook a series of lectures and book signings to help market my first real estate tome, I found most people wanted to hear reassurance about their inclinations to make an investment in real estate. They had land they wanted to buy, a concept for investment but most of all they wanted to buy a house, fix it up, and sell it. Most of them had heard about these seminars offering tips on how to buy a house with no money down or how to flip properties.

Although I don't believe in either of those methodologies, I tried not to be too negative and attempted to impart key, prepurchase procedures concerning such necessities as market research. There were two things that concerned me in 75 percent of the situations where my audience held a somewhat fixed idea about what they wanted to do in regard to real estate.

First, they had given no thought to investigating competitive market conditions other than to ascertain nearby properties values. Consequently, they didn't know, for example, if they were to buy a house as a rental investment property, whether an existing glut of apartments in that community would make their purchase difficult to rent and thus unprofitable. They didn't know whether they were buying into an up economy or a down economy.

Second, these novice investors had no concept of the inherent price of capital—what it would cost to borrow, what form the loan would take, and how it would eventually affect the value of the investment. Fortunately, the year of my book, interest rates were still very low, and this gave even the most naive investor a forgiving climate to indulge in outright stupidity.

For investors starting out, venturing into a first property acquisition, the margin of error was relatively wide, considering where interest rates were at the time. Nothing stays the same, obviously, and interest rates would eventually rise, while demand for property would push up pricing. The margin of error would quickly erode with subsequent investments, subsequent leverage, and any change in market conditions. If the financing was expensive, a reversal of fortune for the investor was definitely at hand. This is what the new Donald Trumps didn't understand.

As I mulled over these issues, I came to see I should do a follow-up book on the subject of financing and ancillary necessities such as corporate formations. Unlike my first book, in which many of the people I profiled were household names, the names in the world of real estate finance aren't as well known to the general public. Conversely, if you work in the industry, you will recognize all the people profiled in *Maverick Real Estate Financing*. After all, who is more important to know, another investor or the person who will lend you money?

I spent an unusually long time deciding which chapters should be included, because I came to realize that how the investment is organized is equally as important as how the investment is financed.

Think of these as the *approach* and the *endgame*. The quest for the right kind of real estate financing eventually moves the machinations forward. With luck, a portfolio of investments is created. The process does not end there. Entrepreneurs have continually searched for the most convenient, legal, tax-advantaged vehicle to hold those investments. As much financial engineering goes into the latter as the former.

Finally, there was the question about what to do with William Sanders. I knew I wanted him in the book, but he didn't fit neatly into a real estate financing chapter. In some regards, he really should have been in the first book, because he has been one of the most successful and imaginative real estate investors this country has produced. However, he was not successful in creating a vehicle for holding those investments. He wanted public valuation with what should have remained a private structure. His company, Security Capital Group, was never very well understood by Wall Street, and in the end he dismantled it, but not before creating some of the biggest real estate companies in their individual sectors, such as ProLogis in industrial.

My solution was to create a first chapter about William Sanders that would in many ways sum up all the chapters.

That freed me to do two things. First, I expanded my list of people to be profiled to include developers and real estate entrepreneurs, because they represent the best users of capital and finance tools. Second, I was able to set the book's structure.

The earlier chapters (after the Bill Sanders chapter) involve true real estate finance—how to get the capital necessary to pay for whatever type of investment you want to make. Obviously, there are myriad ways to make that happen, and I tried to cover the most apparent as well as some of the more esoteric, from simple bank loans to agency loans to equity to low-income-housing tax credits. Most of the gentlemen interviewed here would be considered financial guys of one sort or another. This group includes Jack Cohen, Brian Stoffers, Michael Mazzei, David Twardock, and W. P. Carey. Although now known as a developer, Stephen Ross is in this group because of his pioneering use of low-income-housing tax credits, which is a financing mechanism with which he is still associated through cross-corporate relationships.

The middle chapters cover investment strategies based on corporate finance techniques, and the two gentlemen interviewed here are as different as they can be in the real estate world. After decades in real estate investing, Thomas Barrack prefers the opportunity fund structure, while Milton Cooper remains one of the best corporate chieftains in the real estate industry, having built Kimco Realty Corporation into the largest nonmall retail REIT in the country.

The later chapters cover what I call *corporate formations,* essentially different organizational strategies for holding those investments you struggled so hard to find and acquire. Again, this is a mixed bag of individuals. Maury Tognarelli is a true finance guy, whereas Robert Taubman is of the corporate stripe, the chief executive officer of the mall REIT, Taubman Centers Inc. The last fellow in this group is Leo Wells, who splits the difference—part corporate and part finance.

Real estate financiers are not well known, although they are equally important, successful, and wealthy. Also, some of the financiers are not entrepreneurs but corporate employees who, through either hard work or unusual vision, have helped to create new arenas in real estate finance. I had to make room in this book for both kinds of people.

One final note. Lest you think real estate finance is not very important, consider this: It's because of our country's diverse, deep, and inventive ways to create financial products that we have been able to build a commercial real estate industry that is strong, effective, viable, and different from almost all other countries in the world today. Not only have we been able to create individual wealth, but more important, real estate finance has allowed more people to invest in real estate than at any time in world history.

CHAPTER 1

The Most Amazing Real Estate Company Ever–Again!

William Sanders isn't as well known as Donald Trump or Sam Zell, but no single person has created as many important real estate companies as Sanders. Now in his sixties, Sanders is attempting to build one more great dynamo. For better or worse, his new venture won't be anything like Security Capital Group, his fantastic but flawed real estate company that tried to be all things real estate.

When I stepped outside the airport terminal and into the white light of an El Paso morning, I looked around for my ride, which hadn't yet arrived. I must have stood on the curb for a long time, because I drifted into a sunlight-induced somnambulant state of waiting and didn't see the man approach me. "Steve Bergsman?" he asked. I nodded and shook hands, I guess somewhat reluctantly, because he laughed and said, "Don't worry I'm not the FBI."

He easily could have been, because arranging an interview with William Sanders took a lot of work, a lot of time, and probably a full body scan and scrutiny of my personnel records as kept by some secretive governmental organization.

While researching Sanders before my meeting with him, I came across an old story written during his heyday as chief executive of Security Capital Group. It read: "In a business dominated by unabashed self-promoters, Sanders is an oddity. His name doesn't even hang on his small office buildings. There is not a single color photo of him available. He is said to make anyone who works with him— inside the company or out—sign confidentiality agreements. 'We don't want anyone to make off with our ideas. I am shocked at what my competitors say publicly,' he says in a polite phone conversation to explain why he won't be interviewed."[1]

The unheralded and selectively secretive Sanders, who next to the legendary Sam Zell stands as probably the most influential and storied real estate investor in the country, is hard at work on his next project, which has been rumored about in the business press. I was going to get a first peek, which is why I was invited down to El Paso.

While Sanders is more of an investor than a finance wizard, this book is not only about raising capital, but also about corporation formation. Sanders, more than any other real estate maven, has wrestled with choosing the best type of corporate format to hold real estate. His firm, Security Capital Group, a company that was actually a holding company for investments in private real estate companies and other REITs, was neither liked by Wall Street nor understood by the investment public. As efficient as Security Capital might have been in regard to ownership, it turned out that it was much too complicated for outside investors.

After numerous attempts at simplification, Sanders eventually folded his tent. The last of the company was sold to GE Capital, but that wasn't exactly a giveaway: The deal closed at $5.4 billion.

Even if Sanders had then retired, he still would be one of the great men of modern real estate history because of the number of companies he founded and impacted through investments.

The global real estate firm, Jones Lang LaSalle, had part of its beginnings in LaSalle Partners, Ltd., an innovative company founded by Sanders in El Paso, Texas, in 1968, which moved to Chicago in 1970. Then there was, of course, Security Capital, and in creating Security Capital, Sanders also formed the huge multifamily REIT, Archstone-Smith Trust. Soon afterward, in a de novo development, he created the company that would become ProLogis, the largest industrial REIT in the world.

That alone would make a real estate man famous, but it was only a piece of Security Capital's immenseness. Through Security Capital, Sanders created, expanded, or invested in more than a dozen other companies, including CarrAmerica Realty Corp., Storage USA, Inc., Regency Centers Corp., Homestead Village, and BelmontCorp.

All that may eventually pale next to his latest corporate challenge, Verde Realty, based in El Paso.

GETTING ABOUT

The man who tapped me on the shoulder at the El Paso airport was Christopher Lyons, a former Lehman Brothers guy who was now serving as a vice president with Verde Realty. I opened the car door and climbed into the front seat. The driver, a trim, distinguished-looking man, greeted me with an enthusiastic handshake, "Steve, how are you doing?" My driver for the day was going to be William Sanders himself.

As we wheeled into the streets of El Paso, I reached for the bag holding my tape recorders. Whoops. Ground rule number one. I could take notes during our car ride, which was going to be extensive, but I could not record the interview. Hours later, when we were back at his offices I was finally able to turn on the recorder and get Sanders on record.

One of the first questions I asked as I looked around El Paso—it didn't appear much more appealing to me than the first couple of times I visited the city—was why the heck he was there. This would be revealed to me in the course of the car ride, but the simple answer was "lack of," as in lack of competition, lack of capital, lack of REITs. As explained by Sanders, El Paso and Juárez, its sister city on the other side of border, constituted an international metropolitan area of more than 3 million people. Roughly two-thirds of those people were on the Mexican side, but it was obvious that El Paso was showing significant growth as well.

What Sanders meant was that, despite the growth and the significance of the population, El Paso was relatively off the map for national developers. In addition, all that capital currently lubricating the real estate market rarely washed into El Paso. And finally, most of the big REITs didn't have investments in El Paso. The exception being ProLogis, an industrial REIT, but that was to be understood, because the company's first development was in El Paso.

As Sanders saw it, El Paso was almost virgin territory for what he wanted to do with his new Verde Realty, the first hint of which came as we passed a number of what I thought to be handsome-looking ProLogis industrial buildings (some of them were probably constructed when Sanders controlled the company). This day, however, he was somewhat dismissive of them. "These are good buildings, but they are not where I want to be," he said. "Where's that?" I asked. The answer was, not just near the border with Mexico, but right on the border. That's where Verde Realty was going to be.

You have to understand, if there was ever a real estate investment intellectual, it is Sanders. None of his great creations has simply been about making money. They all fulfilled a purpose or need. LaSalle Partners was started to capture the real estate business corporations needed but didn't want to do. This was outsourcing before outsourcing existed. Security Capital was an experiment in real estate ownership. All that might pale in regard to the latest venture, Verde Realty, which was poised to invest in the most unrealized trendline in real estate.

Here's a quick version of what Sanders explained: For many decades, the Midwest reigned as the country's industrial heartland. And although much production has been shipped overseas, the remaining industrial base has been gradually relocating to the southern states near Mexico because of the inexpensive labor on both sides of the border. This, of course, is the old maquiladora concept.

The classic meaning of *maquiladora* is a factory located in a Mexican border town that imports materials and equipment on a duty- and tariff-free basis for assembly or manufacturing.

The maquiladora programs were weakened by the rise of China and its even cheaper labor, but there is something to be said for proximity. As Sanders pointed out, a number of companies that had shifted manufacturing to China were already coming back to the U.S.-Mexico border area to be closer to their North American customer base. On my tour of the outskirts of Juárez, a very large manufacturing facility was being constructed for a company that was moving some operations back to North America from China. This company wasn't closing its China operations, because the shear size of that market demanded a presence there. But some time-sensitive operations and heavy-weight-to-value products destined for the North American marketplace were better suited for the U.S.-Mexico border region.

Sanders contends the U.S. manufacturing that remains in the country will shift more to the border in a great swath stretching from San Diego on the west to Brownsville, Texas, on the east. In between will be some important nodes, such as El Paso–Juárez.

"In U.S. industrial parks, most of the buildings are for bulk distribution," Sanders maintains, "but down here only about 20 percent fall into that category. The rest are incubator, supplier, manufacturing, and customer service centers."

He prophesies that El Paso will become the epicenter for Hispanic business in the country.

After lunch we headed east of the twin cities. The El Paso–Juárez area was tied together by just four border crossings: two within the city, one to the west, and the fourth, called the Zaragoza point of entry, on the outskirts of the population to the east. It was here we encountered the first of Verde Realty's holdings, a number of industrial buildings and land right against the border crossing to be built out for incubator, supplier, distribution, and manufacturing development.

On the U.S. side of the border, Sanders explained once more to me that the most prime land is close to the actual border and as close as possible to an international crossing, which certainly included the Verde Realty holdings. The reasoning was there was much shipping of goods between related facilities on each side of the border. If assembly was done in Juárez, then suppliers and distribution would be out of El Paso. The twin-plant concept has been a feature of maquiladora almost from the beginning because the U.S. "twin" is often used for such tasks as procurement, distribution, marketing, and some high-tech manufacturing.[2]

Sanders believes in the development potential for the whole corridor of border lands, and that means on the Mexico side as well, so as one travels around central Juárez to the east and south where development begins to scatter into the desert landscape, much of the land is undeveloped. However, one can see the expansion already happening as new residential, retail, and industrial developments pop up madly. It's here where Verde Realty has taken a stand, acquiring six tracts, one of which is designated retail, another housing, and the rest (including a tract closer to Juárez Airport) industrial. As we drove along Juárez's International Beltway, through the heart of Verde's holdings, Sanders spread out his left arm, "Within four miles of here, 20,000 to 25,000 homes are being built."

Even closer are the new industrial complexes. Two Verde properties surround the new manufacturing campus, which itself is near a very large Electrolux campus nearing completion.

HUGE DEVELOPMENT: VERDE MICROCOSM

All this is just small potatoes compared to Verde's immense project to the west of El Paso. It's here that Sanders's vision will play out in full. Verde Realty now controls more than 21,000 acres of land surrounding the Santa Teresa port of entry, which was formally dedicated in 1998. The company's land is actually in New Mexico, not Texas, abutting Verde's land to the south in Mexico, a 46,500-acre, to-be-developed project called San Jeronimo, which is owned by Eloy Vallina, a Verde Group director. Verde is coordinating plans for a binational project of enormous scale and importance for both countries.

Santa Teresa was first envisioned as a transportation and industrial hub by a flamboyant developer named Charlie Crowder, who also owned the nearby Santa Teresa Country Club and most of the water rights in the area. The project, more than 22,000 acres, was just too big, and as some people noted, Crowder was a difficult man to deal with. In any case, financial and political problems vexed the development and Crowder filed for bankruptcy.[3]

That's where Christopher Lyons comes in. Remember, he was the fellow who greeted me at the airport. The family of the former Lehman executive and Verde Realty vice president was a major investor in Santa Teresa, and after the bankruptcy they took it over in 1993. Lyons moved to El Paso to run the operation. His family held the property until selling it to Verde Realty a decade later.

Santa Teresa and San Jeronimo will end up as vast mixed-use developments, a border version of Irvine Ranch in Orange County, California. This actually is an important comparison, because Sanders stressed a key issue for Verde: The company will sell no land for short-term gain. Verde Realty will be the master developer and owner of all the land in the development. "I want to sell fully developed lots to small- and medium-sized homebuilders and develop and retain long-term ownership interest in all income-producing commercial properties with our master-planned communities," Sanders exhorts—with gusto. Projects this big and with such Texas-sized objectives will take a lot of capital.

Verde Realty was founded in November 2003 and is the owner of all real estate assets of Verde Group LLC. Among the partners are a group of old Security Capital managers, directors, and investors, including Ronald Blankenship, former vice chairman and chief operating officer of Security Capital Group; Jay Light, dean of Harvard Business School; Ray Hunt, chairman and CEO of Hunt Consolidated; Jack Frazee, former chief operating officer of Sprint; Laurance Fuller, former cochairman of BP Amoco; and business luminaries such as Eric Dobkin, advisory director of Goldman Sachs and former head of equities, and Steve Roth, chairman and CEO of Vornado Realty Trust.[4]

Some came into Verde with checkbook in hand. However, for such long-range developments, capital will have to be long range as

MEET THE MAVERICKS

William Sanders

Birth Date: 1941

Occupation: Cochairman and Co–chief Executive Officer of Verde Realty

Education: BS, economics and Latin American studies, Cornell University

Career Highlights:

- Founded LaSalle Partners Ltd., now Jones Lang LaSalle
- Founded Security Capital Group
- Created Archstone Communities, now Archstone-Smith Trust
- Created Security Capital Industrial Trust, now ProLogis
- Founded Verde Realty

well. Verde Realty is currently, and will in the future, raise additional capital through a series of private placements done via Wall Street. The idea is not to raise a lot of capital all at once and be pressured into using it all immediately, but rather to raise the capital as needed through private placements, with targets of $250 million at each offering.

Sanders didn't think he would have trouble raising capital, and considering his track record, he is probably right. In fact, he alluded to me that he could easily raise much more than he was seeking in his offerings. Strategically, it didn't make sense, so Sanders says he is going to stick to his plan. "We will capitalize in stages," he stresses.

That leaves the question of organizational structure. In the 1990s, many of Security Capital's companies tried the REIT approach. However, for companies as complicated as Security Capital Group and Verde Realty, the REIT wasn't going to work out. Sanders chose instead the master limited partnership, or MLP, sometimes known as the publicly traded partnership.

Says Sanders, Verde Realty is a master limited partnership for the following reasons:

- Verde has none of the constraints in terms of passive or active income that complicate REITs.

- Being a land developer is difficult in a REIT format.

- Verde doesn't have to distribute 90 percent of taxable income as does a REIT.

- With the MLP, Verde can have a conservative dividend policy, reinvest its capital, and grow the company in a healthy way.

As the name implies, the MLP is partnership in form, consisting of a general partner who handles the day-to-day operations and limited partners who provide the investment funding. It is publicly traded and, as with any public corporation, shareholder risk is limited to the investment in the partnership. Unlike the corporation structure, the MLP carries some interesting benefits: For example, it pays income taxes but files a partnership return; the MLP is exempt from taxation if 90 percent or more of the income is "qualifying income" as defined by the IRS; and, since it is traded, it is a liquid investment. It should also be noted that MLP agreements provide that if the general partner is able to build the business and its returns, the distributions to the general partners may increase in terms of their percentage of the whole, a strong incentive to the general partner to grow income.[5]

That is what Sanders intends for Verde. "We are going to be the dominant real estate developer creating new communities and thoughtful, planned environments in the U.S.-Mexico border region, from San Diego to Texas," he says confidently.

EL PASO TO CHICAGO

Marty Robbins's famous song begins this way: "Out in the west Texas town of El Paso . . ." Bill Sanders's story begins the same way. As a youth he grew up in El Paso. Except for some stints in other cities, he has always come back to his roots.

His first shot at leaving El Paso was college, and he shipped off to Cornell University in upstate New York. That was followed by some Peace Corp–type summer programs that acquired land for agricultural co-ops in Central America. It must have been interesting work because when he arrived back home he joined a local real estate company. His fist job was selling lots to builders, but he soon graduated to managing the preparation of building sites. "It was something I knew nothing about," he reminisces, "which was running six to eight pieces of earth-moving equipment."

Then he moved to another real estate company, where he spent the majority of his time traveling around the western United States looking for motel sites. The best part of the job was meeting others in the real estate brokerage business, especially those who worked for big companies like Coldwell Banker (now CB Richard Ellis) and Grubb & Ellis. This was in the late 1960s, and the very sharp Sanders observed that the real estate industry lacked professionalism and questioned why it couldn't be run with the expertise of a company like Merrill Lynch. He tried to get his own bosses to move along these lines, but they wouldn't bite, so in 1968 Sanders talked four investors into bankrolling a new company called International Development Corp. "I didn't have any money, so each investor/director put up $25,000," says Sanders. "They each got 25,000 shares, and basically we were off to the races."

IDC was a successful real estate company from the start, and that caught the eye of another local developer who was doing construction work around the globe. He pitched Sanders an opportunity. Sanders's associate had a contact in Chicago who wanted to develop regional shopping centers for Montgomery Ward, so in 1970 Sanders moved to Chicago. As it turned out, the Montgomery Ward work never panned out, but there were a number of Fortune 500 companies in the Chicago area, and the ever-insightful Sanders spotted opportunity.

The first thing he did was change the name of his firm. No one knew what IDC stood for, so he created an entirely new moniker, LaSalle Partners, Ltd., because he wanted the name to sound more like an investment bank.

Second, he went after the corporate business. "In that era, big companies had 24 percent of their balance sheet in real estate, and it was totally unmanaged. I felt there was opportunity," he remarks.

Chicago was home to a number of big real estate brokerage and development companies, so to carve out a slice of business Sanders had to be different. Most real estate brokerages were deal shops, and people in the business worked on commissions. He decided LaSalle Partners would be a true service company and that his key employees would be on salary. "We lost a meaningful number of employees, but we were able to attract a totally different caliber of individuals," he says, "This allowed us to be highly professional and service the customer in a strategic and thoughtful way."

LaSalle Partners was so successful it became the second-largest property manager in the United States.

In the late 1980s, Sanders noticed a change in the real estate world. There was a lot of capital flowing into the industry, and the future, he surmised, would be dominated by two phenomena: public capital and specialized operating companies. Sanders wanted to move into the next stage, and at that point he had to decide whether to turn LaSalle Partners into something different or start again.

In 1988, he cashed out of LaSalle Partners (which in 1999 merged with Jones Lang Wootten to form Jones Lang LaSalle) and pocketed, according to the financial press, $20 million.[6] He actually retired as CEO from the company on the last day of 1989.

By 1988, the U.S. real estate markets convulsed. According to myth, Bill Sanders was smart enough to see the recession coming and get out ahead of the crash. The truth, he says, is that he saw change coming, but it wasn't the recession; it was a market shift regarding ownership of commercial real estate in the future. Instead of big commercial real estate remaining in private hands, it would be gathered in by publicly traded organizations. "I wanted to play a key role in that," he says.

Almost from the day he left LaSalle Partners, Sanders threw himself into the task of creating Security Capital—although the real estate world was by this time deep in the doldrums.

THE GRAND EXPERIMENT

Security Capital Group, officially based in Santa Fe, New Mexico— a day's drive from the old Sanders homestead in El Paso—was a tantalizing combination of fantastic success and disappointing failure. The company did everything Sanders intended it do when it was created, but Security Capital never captured the munificence of Wall Street or the attention of retail investors. Security Capital Group went public in 1997 at $28 a share, and just four years later sold to

THE MOST AMAZING REAL ESTATE COMPANY EVER—AGAIN! **15**

GE Capital at $26 a share—a 25 percent premium over its closing price when the deal was announced. Like many public real estate companies at that time, the stock for the most part traded below its opening share price and sometimes at a full 30 percent discount off the underlying value of the company.[7]

Not that it was a grim and painful experience. The GE Capital deal was valued at $5.4 billion. If Sanders failed, then he definitely failed upward, considering the original company was capitalized at about $108 million.

"People referred to us as a holding company or a conglomerate of real estate, and that hurt us in the public markets," says Sanders. Still, Sanders makes it clear that Security Capital's investment in individual firms "did not hurt the companies in which we were the principal shareholders."

By all accounts, Security Capital was truly an amazing concept, the likes of which we probably will never see again.

The idea behind it was that Security Capital would buy controlling interests in small real estate companies or create entirely new companies. These companies would then become, through hard work and investment, the dominant leaders in their focused real estate space. Some of the individual companies would also be REITs. Organizationally, it would be Security Capital Group at the top, and below would be other companies and REITs, all unrelated, in which Security Capital owned a controlling interest.

Eventually, it became much more complicated than that, with Security Capital Group owning some companies directly, some of which were holders of other companies, and in addition maintaining a controlling interest in an overseas investment company, which also owned companies. Within all that mass were operating companies, management companies, and a European group that owned interest in a different set of operating companies.

When I asked Sanders about being based in Santa Fe, which was relatively isolated, at least in terms of air connections and access to capital, he replied that he was rarely there, having spent most of his time traveling to places like London, the domicile of Security Capital's European company.

This was all a bit later. In the beginning, he had to find a way to capitalize his great scheme.

Sanders always thought big, which meant he needed big money. His first estimate for Security Capital was a mere $150 million in capitalization. To get that funding, he put together a private placement memorandum (used to raise growth and expansion capital by issuing stock in accordance with Securities and Exchange Commission), and for investment dollars Sanders turned to many of the companies he had dealt with at LaSalle Partners.

"We brought in 13 institutions, and every single investor, with the exception of one, thought I was nuts about real estate being securitized," Sanders recalls. "It was a gentleman by the name of Peter Lincoln, who ran a key part of the U.S. Steel pension fund, who bought into my strategy. None of the other companies did, but they knew I was a hard worker and I was putting money in on the same basis, which was the only reason they came in."

There were some blips. Prudential wanted to put in $90 million, but as the money was being raised, Kuwait was invaded by Iraq which set off war, and the big insurer cut its investment down to $25 million because of uncertain times. Other insurance companies, such as Allstate and Aon, maintained their positions.

"On the last day of the year 1990 we closed with over $108 million," says Sanders.

The company's first deal was the acquisition of a controlling interest in (no surprise here) an El Paso–based REIT called Property Trust of America, which had a little piece of everything: retail, industrial, multifamily, and hotels. Sanders and the new Security Capital management team sold off everything except multifamily and created Security Capital Pacific Trust, a Denver-based West Coast apartment developer and manager. For the East Coast, Security Capital Atlantic Inc. was created from scratch.

In 1998, when Sanders and his management team started simplifying the company, he merged the two entities into a new company called Archstone Communities. Today, the company is Archstone-Smith Trust, the second largest multifamily REIT in the country, with a total market capitalization of $12.1 billion. (Also in 1998, he merged two shopping center companies in which Security Capital was the major stockholder, Regency Realty Group and Pacific Realty Trust. Today, Regency Centers Corporation is the fifth-largest shopping center owner, with a total market capitalization of $5.4 billion.)[8]

Early in the 1990s, Security Capital began in El Paso by developing an industrial park, and this small development became the basis of Security Capital Industrial Trust. It went public in the mid-1990s when it had a value of about $250 million. In 1998, the firm changed its name to ProLogis, which today is the world's largest holder of industrial properties. Its total market capitalization at midyear 2005 reached $12.5 billion.

That was about as simple as it got for Security Capital. It created a holding company in Europe called Security Capital U.S. Realty and took that public. Although it was Europe-based, it owned U.S. operations. For example, when Sanders shifted from just creating companies to buying into existing REITs, this was done through this company, which was eventually known as SC-U.S. Realty. In the mid-1990s, SC-U.S. Realty bought a controlling interest in CarrAmerica Realty Corp., an office/industrial REIT, Storage USA, and Regency Centers.

Security Capital went public in 1997, and due in large measure to the dot-com bubble, the stock price slumped along with all real estate–related stocks at that time.

Sanders had built the company he wanted, a securitized real estate venture that owned controlling interests in other real estate companies, some publicly traded, some not. Unfortunately, no one else bought into this vision. The stock drifted downward. Wall Street viewed Security Capital as a holding company; investors never quite understood what they were supposed to be buying into. Security Capital had become a hydra-headed monster. By 1999, Sanders realized he had created a complex structure of unrealized value, and he began to dismantle it.

Before that happened, when Security Capital was at its apex, it was for a moment the most amazing real estate company ever created.

In a very simplified schematic the company looked like this: At the top was Security Capital Group and it stood on two legs, the largest of which consisted of directly owned companies, including Archstone (multifamily), ProLogis (industrial), Homestead (hotels), BelmontCorp (senior housing), Strategic Hotel Capital, SC-Capital Management Group, and SC-European Realty. The last was itself a holding company for companies such as Access Storage Solutions, Interparking, EuroOffice, City & West End, and London & Henley.

The smallest leg of the company was no slouch, a separate publicly traded company, SC-U.S. Realty. It included controlling interest in CarrAmerica, Storage USA, Regency, plus CWS Communities, InterPark, Center Retail Trust, and other assorted special-opportunity investments.

Since Wall Street had a bias against holding companies, Sanders decided to first combine similar operations within the company. When those maneuvers failed to lift the stock, he opted to dismantle some of it.

In a 1999 management letter, Sanders wrote under the header, "simplifying structure to eliminate the public/private discount and clarify public market perception," that he would simplify Security Capital's structure and create a valuable currency in the stock "by making it the best way to invest in our family of outstanding, high-growth real estate operating companies."[9]

An analyst who followed Security Capital noted, "Security Capital's goal is to try and make the company appear less complex in nature. We understand Security Capital's goal of simplifying its structure—intelligently reducing the number of public and private investments it holds to become a cleaner company that is easier to understand."[10]

The analyst concluded that the new structure would allow investors to make easier decisions on an investment in Security Capital. They could invest in Security Capital Group or in one or more of the six companies it controlled on the New York Stock Exchange.

First, Security Capital Group bought its affiliate, SC-U.S. Realty for $1.4 billion; then, over the next two years it sold Archstone, privatized Homestead, sold Strategic Hotel Capital, sold City & West End, sold London & Henley, sold City Center Retail Trust, and got rid of most of its opportunistic investments under the old SC-U.S. Realty.

In 2001, analysts estimated Security Capital held combined assets valued at $17.2 billion, but it continued to dismantle. That year, Homestead Village, the extended-stay lodging company, was sold for $740 million to an affiliate of Blackstone Real Estate Advisors.

Then it was all gone, much faster than it was acquired.

In the post–September 11 environment, a group of executives representing different industries met in New York on September 25. Sanders attended, representing the real estate world. The one executive who impressed Sanders the most, basically because of his optimism, was General Electric's chairman and chief executive Jeff Immelt. After the dinner was over, Immelt and Sanders made small talk.

Immelt must have been impressed with Sanders, because soon

afterward he received a call from General Electric offering to buy his company. At first Sanders thought the price too low, but he eventually negotiated a price that was appropriate for Security Capital Group shareholders.

"General Electric was one of the few companies in the world that could pay cash for us," says Sanders, "and they paid a fair price."

A TRUE MAVERICK'S APPROACH TO REAL ESTATE

1. Deciding on the best type of organizational format depends on what the company is trying to accomplish. One size does not fit all.
2. Don't make your company too complicated for investors to understand. Keep structure simple.
3. Look for "lack ofs": locations where there is a *lack of* competition, *lack of* capital, *lack of* other big companies, and so on.
4. Get ahead of the trends in your industry.
5. Look at demographics, which often point to the regions that need real estate investment.
6. Although not in vogue, don't be afraid of building structures for the manufacture of goods. Just make sure it is in a region where the workforce maintains a competitive advantage.
7. Opportunities abound outside the U.S. borders.
8. Real estate is a long-term investment. Think long term.
9. Don't try to raise too much capital at one time, because the pressure to invest it quickly is overwhelming.
10. Big enough? An alternative to the REIT structure is a master limited partnership.
11. If your company is not structured properly to compete, don't be afraid to make radical changes.
12. If your company is not structured properly to compete, don't be afraid to sell out and start again.
13. When raising capital, think big.
14. If you capitalize through Wall Street, be aware of the financial market's particular pressures, biases, and limitations.

CHAPTER 2

Real Estate Loans

Whether it's for development, redevelopment, or acquisition, lenders now offer such a wide variety of loans that it's easy to get confused. To make matters worse, almost every project has to layer in different types of debt. It is never just one loan. At minimum, expect to go through at least two different and separate loan processes.

If you want to get a loan to buy a house, you would probably turn to your local mortgage broker, who can easily arrange the financing for you. If all goes well, you go to the office, sign a bunch of documents, and presto, you have the money to acquire your dream house. Basically, it is a one-loan, one-step process. The same is true for other big purchases such as a cars. It just takes one loan.

The residential loan process is very efficient, formulaic, and, except for price, rarely negotiable. In commercial real estate, the process can be—and usually is—a lot more complicated. The commercial lending process is inefficient, customized, and highly negotiable.

Rarely in the commercial real estate process does one loan do the job. Let's say you live in Orange County, California, and you decide to build a small office building about 10 miles down the road from your home. You expect the cost to be around $1 million, and it will take at least two separate loans to make it happen. To build, you have to get a construction loan. When the building is up and functioning with tenants, you have to find a permanent loan to, in effect, take out the construction loan.

Two loans are good, because the financing of that small office building could easily get a lot more intense. Sometimes the loan to acquire the land is separate from the construction loan, which means getting two loans before the building is open for business. After it opens, let's say a local mortgage banker is willing to do a permanent loan, but at only a 70 percent loan-to-value ratio, which will cover $700,000 of the cost. In hand, you have enough capital for $100,000 of the remaining $300,000. So you find a mezzanine loan for $200,000, or that 20 percent piece of the capital that was missing. For your project you have now signed for four different loans.

Even that is a simple financing, because capital sources can slice and dice the loan process so many different ways. This is not done to confuse you, but because lenders have a job to do, and that is to get capital into the marketplace, which is not as easy as it seems, as all other lenders are trying to do the very same thing. As a result, capital sources engineer a variety of lending constructs to create a competitive edge and to best serve people like you who want to invest in real estate.

Competition is not the only reason for the vast array of loan types available. Capital sources need to lend, but they want to do so with minimum risk. Much of the layering involved in financing a commercial real estate project is done to mitigate risk. Instead of writing 100 percent loan-to-value on an apartment complex, the lender would rather share the risk with the developer and, perhaps, another institution that will provide a mezzanine loan. In addition, with the advent of securitized lending in the 1990s, real estate is also about risk shift. Whether you are the landlord, tenant, buyer, or seller, you essentially take the risk you are comfortable with and pay someone else to take the risk that you are not comfortable with. Investors buy the piece of risk that they treasure.

In 2004, Newcastle Partners, a Newport Beach commercial real estate investment and development firm, bought two vacant buildings in Irvine, California, totaling 150,000 square feet of industrial space. To make the deal happen, Newcastle turned to Chicago-based Cohen Financial LP, an investment bank that works solely in commercial real estate finance. Acting as a mortgage banker, Cohen Financial arranged a two-year bridge loan (used short term until permanent financing put in place) from an insurer. The loan, in addition to providing acquisition funds, included a construction component that allowed Newcastle to upgrade and re-tenant.

After the properties were acquired, the company secured a major, Class A tenant for the larger of the two buildings. That meant having to convert the old warehouse structure into a modern office building. Since the 15-year lease increased the property's value,

Newcastle secured a redevelopment loan from Cohen Financial that refinanced the bridge loan, covered construction costs, and paid the now-higher leasing commissions.

Newcastle still wasn't done. When construction was completed and the tenant in place, Newcastle sold the smaller building and then arranged permanent financing for the development. In the end, Newcastle received from Bear Stearns, the New York investment bank, a five-year, fixed-rate, interest-only loan.

The deal for the permanent loan was actually even more complex, I simplified it for the sake of an example.

It's almost foolhardy to try to list all the loans that can be involved in a major development. Lenders come up with new products all the time, many of which become adopted by the industry in general. This chapter concentrates only on the basic loans: construction, bridge, hard money, permanent, and mezzanine.

THE CONSTRUCTION LOAN

In commercial real estate, nothing is as easy as it appears. First of all, this type of loan can carry different names, depending on what the loan covers. A simple construction loan includes these characteristics:

- *Coverage.* Construction or property improvements.

- *Collateral.* Land and the improvements.

- *Reserve.* Construction reserve accounts maintained to disburse capital during the course of construction. Interest is paid out of the reserve account.

- *Contingency.* One recommendation is that the proposed budget include a certain amount of contingency reserve for cost changes during the construction process.[1]

- *Interest.* Usually established as interest-only for the construction periods. Amortization required once units (office, apartment development) are sold. The interest reserve should be accounted for in the budget as part of the total costs.[2]

To sum up, the construction loan is a short-term line of credit used to pay for the materials and labor required to build the project. Money is advanced to the builder as construction progresses. Borrowers pay interest on the amount; payments are based on the outstanding balance on the line of credit; and payments are lower at the beginning, but increase monthly as the builder draws down on the credit line. The costs associated with a construction loan can be more than that of a traditional mortgage if the lender doesn't force the borrower to come up with more equity.[3]

As noted, construction loans can include land acquisition, so for this stage of the project the loan can take on a number of different formats, all with slightly different purposes. Sometimes, the financing is called a *ground-up loan,* because proceeds are used for the purpose of a ground-up construction project, including purchase of land. The construction period will usually last up to nine months at interest-only. The lender often includes interim interest and construction contingency costs within the loan amount. What is interesting about this loan is, once the construction period is completed, the loan morphs automatically into a permanent loan.[4]

Then there are the simple acquisition loans, which as the name implies are used to buy property. This loan can go deeper into the process, becoming an acquisition and development loan (sometimes known just as a development loan). Hence the money can be used to buy the property and develop it. For this type of loan, the loan-to-value ratio is determined by the estimated improvement value.[5]

While qualitatively there doesn't appear to be too much of a difference between the acquisition and acquisition and development loan, the lending specifics can be very different, even from the same lender.

Here's how one lender approached the financing on an acquisition and acquisition and development loan. Allbex Financial Partners in Newport Beach, California, advertised acquisition loan size for commercial property at $1 million to $50 million, variable- and fixed-interest rates, purchases to 80 percent of purchase price, and amortization to 30-year schedules. However, on its acquisition and development loan, the format shows 75 percent plus-or-minus loan-to-cost (borrowing to cost of construction) or 80 percent plus-or-minus loan-to-value (expected value of project), whichever is less; two- to three-year plus-or-minus loan term for the construction, mini-perm loan to stabilize the project, and permanent financing at the end.[6]

THE BRIDGE LOAN

Let's say you received your construction loan and began work on your development, the small office building. However, things are not going as well as you planned, and the bank that gave you the construction loan calls and says, "You need to pay this thing down." You don't have that kind of capital now, but leasing is beginning to take off, so you turn to another lender that will do a bridge loan.

Essentially, a bridge loan carries the investor or developer until permanent financing can be put into place—it bridges the cash gap! It's a short-term loan and solves the problem of that sticky situation in which the construction lender wants a paydown but the income stream hasn't kicked into place to get a permanent loan. On a more positive note, the bridge loan can be used for a timely acquisition or business opportunity because it allows an investor to act quickly. The bridge loan can be used for acquisitions, buyouts, foreclosures, cash-outs, and construction purposes. Bridge loans are easiest to get for income-producing properties.[7]

Charlotte, North Carolina–based Mountain Funding early in 2005 handled a number of bridge loans. It closed a $23.25 million bridge loan for St. Andrews at the Polo Club, a 200-unit condominium complex in Wellington, Florida, and a $41.5 million bridge loan for a 380-unit apartment complex in Naples, Florida, slated for conversion into a condo development. On the first deal with St. Andrews at the Polo Club, Mountain Funding noted at the time the existing loan was refinanced with a bridge loan that permits distributions to borrower from net sales—as long as the sales continued as projected. The idea was to help the developer extract equity from the project so he could secure another condominium project.[8]

Cohen Financial is another company that does bridge loan financing. Jack Cohen, its chief executive officer, explained to me that his company approaches this kind of funding by looking at the business plan of the borrower and determining how solid it is and how talented the principals are in executing the plan. Plus, says Cohen, his company has raised funds from investors for bridge loans. In essence, Cohen Financial holds an available pool of capital because bridge loans need to be turned around very quickly.

Cohen gave me this scenario where a bridge loan would be necessary: A developer in Des Moines, Iowa, secured a Class A tenant for an office building he was constructing. The Class A tenant unfortunately couldn't move fast enough to sign a lease because of one internal problem after another. As a developer, you know the Class A tenant will be coming on board, but your construction loan is due. The bank of Des Moines wants its money. Most bridge lenders would take a serious look at a situation such as that.

Bridge loans can be used creatively in a financing scheme. As an example, when Wells Fargo announced plans to vacate its space in an 80-year-old San Francisco office building, an investment group

MEET THE MAVERICKS

Jack Cohen

Birth Date: 1957

Occupation: Chief Executive Officer, Cohen Financial LP

Education: BA, liberal arts, Claremont College; BS, civil engineering, Stanford University; MS, construction engineering, Stanford University

Career Highlights:

- Refinanced and reoriented Cohen Financial
- Devised three-unit (agency, advisor, principal) structure for company
- Made company into one of the largest originators of commercial real estate finance loans
- Divested Cohen Capital

decided to buy the property cheaply and then renovate the structure back into a Class A property. Cohen Financial secured $40 million to finance a portion of the acquisition costs, enabling the investors to get control of the property. Eighteen months later, the investors obtained through Cohen Financial a $58 million bridge loan to repay the original loan and provide capital for the renovation and repositioning the balance of the property.

Bridge loans can also be used for acquisitions. Here's how it works:

- A bridge loan is secured on the property. In effect, it is a mortgage, but without the preferential mortgage rate of interest. Interest rates are quoted per month, normally around 2.5 percent above the base rate.[9]

- One suggestion is to go through the bridge loan preapproval process to see how much of a loan you can qualify for. With preapproval, an investor can act quickly.

- Most applicants will be asked to secure the loan with collateral, which might include the property involved in the purchasing process.

- Expect to pay a slightly higher rate of interest for this short-term loan.

- The maximum term for a bridge loan for acquisition purposes is often 24 months.[10]

THE HARD MONEY LOAN

This is a form of bridge loan, or gap financing. Like the bridge loan, it is short term and used when time is of the essence. Sometimes this loan process can be completed in just a little more than a week's time.

The major difference between the usual bridge loan and a hard money loan is that in the latter instance, it is considered a "nonbankable loan," or sometimes a "private money loan."

These loans fall outside the underwriting guidelines of conventional sources such as banks or conduits and are often used in the following circumstances: quick funding for time-sensitive loans, loss of a bank loan, borrower deciding to avoid a bank loan, and borrower or property having circumstances that make it difficult to obtain a bank loan.[11]

Here are some important considerations with a hard money loan:

- There is some flexibility, as these loans are available on entitled and untitled land, residential and commercial developments, income-producing properties, or partner buyouts.

- Value of the property is the primary qualification.

- They are available on projects where the investor has significant equity in the collateral regardless of bad credit history.

- They are more expensive than bank loans.[12]

THE PERMANENT LOAN

At some point, when the construction on your new building has been completed and the tenants have begun to move in, it will be time to replace the construction loan with what is called a *permanent loan,* which is nothing more than a long-term mortgage.

The thing to remember about permanent financing is that it is most commonly used on stabilized properties where there is sufficient cash flow. Amortizations can be anywhere from 5 to 30 years, while interest rates vary depending on the credit quality of the borrower, property type, location, and current market conditions. Nonrecourse financing (debt for which the borrower is not personally liable) is available for most borrowers and product types.[13]

As with all loans, there is a process to go through.

Here's how one company describes its procedures: For initial quote, borrower should submit the appropriate loan submission form, three years of income and expense statements, three years of occupancy history, and a tri-merged credit report with bureau scores for each principal. If the quote is acceptable, a borrower conference call to confirm that terms and conditions are acceptable will take place. A letter of interest will then be issued disclosing proposed terms, conditions, estimated costs, and documentation required for underwriting. An application fee of $2,500 is required upon acceptance of the letter of interest. Upon review of all requested documentation, site inspection, and preliminary underwriting approval, a formal application will be issued. A deposit to cover these expenses and a good faith deposit of 0.5 percent of the proposed loan amount is required at application. This good faith deposit may be credited toward the commitment fee listed if the loan application is approved. If the loan application is denied, this good faith deposit will be refunded to the applicant.[14]

While the process may be rigid, the permanent loan is extremely flexible. Interest can be variable or fixed and can be twisted to fit the specific financing needs of the property. Lenders compete for these loans and are generally willing to customize if necessary.

Here are some examples of permanent loan financing:

- *Ten-year, interest free.* In Clifton Park, New York, CIBC World Markets in 2005 closed an $18 million first-mortgage permanent loan secured by a fee-simple interest in Shopper's World Shopping Center. The loan was structured with a 10-year term and is interest-only for the first two years, with a 30-year amortization schedule.[15]

- *Cash flow increase.* In Atlanta, Robert Realty Investors Inc. in 2005 closed a $21 million permanent loan to refinance the 285-unit second phase of its Addison Place apartment community. The company used the new loan and $1.1 million of its own working capital to pay off an existing $22.1 million loan. The new loan, fixed for 10 years, lowers the interest rate from 8.62 percent to 6.35 percent, allowing cash flow from the property to increase by $500,000 per year.[16]

- *Refinance.* In 2004, Pacific Security Capital secured an $8.85 million permanent financing for an Albany, Georgia, shopping center.

The first mortgage had a "competitive" spread over the 10-year Treasury from a conduit for which Pacific Security is a correspondent. The loan allowed the shopping center owner to refinance an acquisition and development loan to lock in low rates.[17]

Commercial mortgages are long-term loans that the borrower is required to pay on a monthly basis. The property and the land serve as collateral and a reminder to the borrower that payments have to be made. If the borrower cannot or will not make the payments, the lender can take the property through foreclosure.[18]

THE MEZZANINE LOAN

The basic mezzanine loan is a filler. When your primary lender will go only 80 percent loan-to-value and you are sitting there with enough capital for another 10 percent, that still leaves you short 10 percent of the final cost. The mezzanine loan fills that space.

Even if the investor had the capital for the remaining 20 percent of the cost, he or she might still opt for the mezzanine loan to use the extra capital for another investment. While a first-mortgage lender will typically only lend 70 or 80 percent of a project's cost, investors tend to want to reduce their own equity contribution to a fraction of that cost.[19]

"It should be compared to a home equity loan," says Cohen. "[*Mezzanine* is] a French term and implies a 50/50 relationship on the equity invested in the deal."

To fully appreciate the mezzanine loan's position in your borrowings, think of all the participants in the capital structure as one stack. On the bottom is the primary mortgage, then sitting on top of that is the mezzanine loan, and finally at the very top is the equity, or your position. Indeed, *stack* is a common reference, and it is used because, in the case of default, the lender in the bottom position has first rights, followed by the next lender in the stack.

The first-mortgage lender's capital is always the largest component of a project's capital stack because it is the cheapest. The cost of a mezzanine loan is much higher than that of a first mortgage. Even if the interest rate on a first mortgage is in the low or middle single digits, rates on the mezzanine could easily be double digits. In addition, the mezzanine debt is often secured by an assignment of equity interest in the mortgage borrower.[20] To put it another way, if Bob & Friends Investments LLC is the investment or borrowing entity, the mezzanine loan might be secured by 100 percent of the voting stock of Bob & Friends Investments.

Important reference points on a mezzanine loan are as follows:

- It is a totally separate loan from a first mortgage.

- It is made to the parent entity of the real estate borrower; hence the note is secured with pledge of equity interest in the borrower.

- It has its own borrower, its own promissory note, separate loan documents, and separate collateral.

- It is largely nonrecourse.

- Prepayment terms might be comparable to a mortgage loan counterpart.[21]

- It should pay higher yields.

- It is constructed so that the lender's rights are terminated upon repayment.

- The mezzanine loan often includes substantial fees.

Although lenders had been pushing mezzanine loans quite hard in the first years of this new century, when I caught up with Jack

Cohen in the spring of 2005 and asked him about the product, he frankly said that from a lender's viewpoint he wouldn't do it. His quote exactly: "I wouldn't be on the mezzanine side right now as a lender."

He just didn't like the real estate brick-and-mortar fundamentals prevalent in certain geographies and product types. "If we have a devaluation in the marketplace, mezzanine will get crunched." The ironic part of Cohen's declaration is that his company, Cohen Financial, offers mezzanine loans, as well as bridge loans, construction loans, and industrial equity.

STICK TO YOUR KNITTING

Cohen Financial, a large, entrepreneurial mortgage and real estate investment banking firm, was formed by Benjamin "Buddy" Cohen, one of the more interesting real estate pioneers, who is still alive today and swinging deals from his retirement home in Palm Springs, California.

Back in 1965, Buddy Cohen formed BB Cohen in Chicago. It was at the time the first correspondent mortgage banker in the country. That came about because Union Mutual of Portland, Maine, like other insurance companies, used its capital for real estate investments. However, since the insurance companies often didn't staff lending offices, it created "correspondents" that represented them in various locations. This was essentially how the real estate finance industry was built: Independent mortgage banking companies were the bridge between capital sources and borrowers.

BB Cohen was so successful that the company attracted the attention of another Chicago firm called Walter B. Heller that wanted to go into the real estate business. It bought BB Cohen in 1972. Almost 30 years later, General Electric acquired Heller.

Somewhere along the line Buddy Cohen decided he wanted to be

MEET THE MAVERICKS

Benjamin "Buddy" Cohen

Birth Date: 1929
Occupation: Founder, Cohen Financial
Education: BA, finance, University of Wisconsin
Career Highlights:

- Founded BB Cohen, first commercial mortgage banker
- Sold BB Cohen to Walter B. Heller
- Founded Cohen Financial
- Oversaw real estate workout of Westinghouse and Focus Financial

an entrepreneur again instead of working for someone else, so in 1978 he started another company, called Cohen Financial, a mortgage banking firm.

By this time there were quite a number of mortgage banking firms in the country. These were boom years for real estate and everyone was doing well, so much so that a number of mortgage bankers decided they would get into the development and investment business. Buddy Cohen, a finance guy, stuck to his area of expertise: He built retained earnings, got bank lines, and became a direct lender (using Cohen Financial capital as opposed to someone else's capital).

As it turned out, it was a smarter way to do business, because when the real estate market convulsed in the late 1980s, the mortgage bankers who wandered away from the core business got crunched. During the real estate recession that lasted into the early 1990s, there wasn't a lot of lending being done, but Cohen Financial still had capital and stayed in business.

TRIANGULAR APPROACH TO REAL ESTATE FINANCE

After graduating from high school, Jack Cohen went west to California, first with a sojourn at Claremont College and then at Stanford University. Cohen didn't go to the West Coast to spend his days in idyllically surfing at the beach or mellowing out at Big Sur. He studied. By the time he finished his schooling, Jack Cohen had two bachelor's degrees, one in liberal arts from Claremont and one in civil engineering from Stanford, and a master's degree in construction management from Stanford. After years of working as a dispute resolution consultant to the construction industry (his specialty was construction productivity processes), Cohen finally succumbed to his father's many attempts to get him to come home to the family business. The year was 1981.

Jack Cohen started in the family firm as a loan officer, eventually headed production, and in 1990 became president of the business. In 1998, Jack Cohen decided to take the business in a new direction. His father retired, and he became chief executive officer. Jack's brother, Bruce Cohen, took the title of chief investment officer.

By the middle of the 1990s, Jack Cohen began to rethink the business. First, he could see a necessity for doing business beyond just local mortgage banking, and second, a lot of corporate and institutional businesses required different skill sets than those that could normally be found among finance providers.

"In the early 1990s everyone saw the business as a random collection of transactions," recalls Jack Cohen. "We saw it as a business that could be run like a business, a distribution channel representing users and providers of capital. The distribution model was bidirectional and lubricated by our own capital."

He adds, "Some mortgage bankers might say they are representing the borrower, others the lenders, but our view was that we were representing the transactions based on what role we were playing: a consultant, a broker, or a principal. You could reduce origination costs by selling the customer multiple products through multiple roles."

Jack Cohen envisioned and then created a real estate investment firm with three strategies: (1) As an agent, or mortgage banker, the company sources real estate loans; (2) as an advisor, Cohen Financial provides clients with market perspectives; and (3) as a principal, the firm provides access to financing, manages investments, and acquires income property.

"We decided this business model made sense, and we tested it by opening in 1995 an office in Madison, Wisconsin." Two years later, Cohen sought out legendary real estate investors such as Sam Zell and William Sanders to bank the growth of the company, but no one else saw the efficacy of the format. Nevertheless, in 1998, Cohen Financial was refinanced and became Cohen Financial LP. The company raised $80 million, which it leveraged with $300 million in bank loans, and then proceeded to grow like wildfire.

In 1998 alone, the company opened offices in Los Angeles, Houston, Tampa, and Washington, D.C. In 1999, Cohen Financial shifted its growth strategy to expand by acquisitions, nabbing E.S. Merriman & Sons in San Francisco, Harbor Financial Commercial Real Estate Services in Sacramento and Denver, and West Coast Mortgage & Investment Banking in Portland.[22] Today the company manages 11 offices in 10 major cities around the country.

In 1995, the company counted $300 million of origination and $300 million in servicing. By 2000, Cohen Financial could brag of $2 billion in origination and $3 billion in servicing. Today, Cohen

Financial is recognized as one of the nation's largest originators of commercial real estate loans, with about $4 billion in transactions and $5 billion in loan servicing. The company has also provided advisory services on more than $1 billion in assets.

In June 2004, Cohen Financial made another big change. Using a $700 million capitalization, it spun off Cohen Capital, which was the investment arm of the company. "We took that business, which was doing about $300 million in direct lending, and spun it off into a money management group," Jack Cohen explains. "We had total investment of over $1.1 billion, never had a delinquency, and boasted a 20 percent internal rate of return on our equity. That business was capital-constrained, however, and other Cohen Financial businesses are not. Cohen Capital needed capital; Cohen Financial did not. By launching that business on its own, we were able to recapitalize the business."

Bruce Cohen, Jack's brother, became CEO of Cohen Capital. All shareholders of Cohen Financial also have shares in Cohen Capital. "Cohen financial remains with its historic shareholder base, engaged in the service businesses it has historically been engaged in—debt and equity placement, investment brokerage, loan servicing—while Cohen Capital will continue the investment activity it has been engaged in over the past several years," Jack Cohen told the financial press soon after the spin-off.[23]

Jack Cohen defines Cohen Financial as kind of a one-stop funding shop for first and supplemental capital to the middle market segment (financing up to $20 million). As a direct lender, Cohen Financial's bridge loan (conventional and structured) sits in the range from $3 million to $15 million, construction loans (conventional and credit tenant) from $2 million to $15 million, mezzanine debt from $2 million to $20 million, and industrial equity from $1 million to $10 million.

"Our customer base is primarily entrepreneurial, which we define as a $5 million to $15 million sweet spot," says Cohen. "That said, we have done loans as low as $300,000 and as high as $566 million. We have international customers as well."

In May 2005, Cohen Financial secured almost $20 million in debt financing for three Illinois retail properties. In Cresthill, it closed on a $14 million financing package for a 238,136-square-foot grocery store–anchored property. Terms of the 10-year nonrecourse loan include a 30-year amortization schedule, 70 percent loan-to-value ratio, and pricing based on the 10-year U.S. Treasuries. The lender was a CMBS conduit. In Peoria, Cohen Financial secured $4,125,000 in debt financing on a 120,000-square-foot unanchored neighborhood retail center. Terms of the 10-year nonrecourse loan include a 30-year amortization schedule, 80 percent loan-to-value, and pricing based on the 10-year U.S. Treasuries. The lender was a CMBS conduit. In Chicago, Cohen finalized $1.5 million in debt financing on a 4,380-square-foot single-tenant retail building. Terms of the 10-year nonrecourse loan include a 30-year amortization schedule, 75 percent loan-to-value, and pricing based on the 10-year U.S. Treasuries.

In regard to industrial, Cohen Financial in the past established three investment funds—Acorn Industrial Fund, Acorn Industrial Fund II, and Strategic Equity Fund—for high-net-worth individuals to invest in the sector. "Maybe because we are in Chicago, we have always felt the best product for investment was industrial," Cohen explains. "It has the lowest risk and it's very stable. We have been aggressive in terms of lending for speculative space and we also found we like to buy this stuff, so we raised money and bought the product."

Acting as an intermediary, the company can deliver a much larger loan because the capital is sourced elsewhere, from life insurance companies, capital market lenders, banks, finance companies, equity investors, and opportunity funds. Again, acting as an agent, the company can propose alternative capital structures, secure a range of quotes, recommend providers of capital, negotiate the loan application, control selection of third-party vendors, negotiate the loan commitment, and help close the loan.

Cohen suggests his company is one of the few, if not the only one, that acts as principal, advisor, and agent for the commercial real estate industry.

"Back in the 1980s when I started, everyone was impressed by the developer who had a big office building," says Cohen. "It kind of bothered me that it was all based on this edifice complex. What also annoyed me was that developers treated their architects like untouchables, their contractors as respected partners, their lawyers and accountants like mentors, and their brokers like shit. So, my view was, I wanted to be known as a financial architect and that we are selling a service."

Cohen continues, "When we sit with customers we are trying to support their strategic initiatives. We believe we get hired to help customers do the job better, faster, and cheaper. It's the creative application of a capital structure and plan that supports our customers once we understand their plan and objectives."

In 2004, Cohen told the financial press, "Most of the mortgage banking industry is selling a product; we want to sell service. We come to a customer with a blank sheet and ask him to tell us his objectives, and then we offer a solution. We fill in the sheet with products and services and let the customer choose. We talk it out with the customer and come back with a capital structure based on business strategy. It's a better deal for us, too, because the customer sees us as serving needs."[24]

A TRUE MAVERICK'S APPROACH TO EQUITY FINANCING

1. Commercial real estate always takes more than one loan.
2. A construction loan can get complex: Is it also an acquisition or an acquisition and development loan?
3. A construction loan is a short-term line of credit used to pay for materials and labor.
4. In a construction loan, money is advanced as work progresses.
5. Construction loan payments increase as the builder draws down credit line.
6. Bridge loans carry investors until permanent financing can be found.
7. Bridge loans can be used for a timely acquisition.
8. A bridge loan is secured by the property involved in the purchasing process.
9. Bridge loans are short term with relatively higher interest rates.
10. Hard money loans fall outside underwriting guidelines of conventional loans.
11. When a bank loan won't or can't do, try a hard money loan.
12. Hard money loans are not cheap.
13. Construction loans are replaced by permanent loans, basically a first mortgage.
14. Look for a permanent loan when the property has stabilized.
15. Despite the permanent loan being very common, the process can be time-consuming.
16. Property and/or land serves as collateral for a permanent loan.

17. Mezzanine loans fill the gap between a first mortgage and an equity position.
18. A mezzanine loan is a totally different product than a permanent loan and often with a different lender.
19. Mezzanine notes are secured by equity interest in the borrower.
20. Watch for hidden fees in mezzanine transactions.

CHAPTER 3

Advantages and Disadvantages of Conduit Loans

Although commonplace now, the conduit loan is just a little over a decade old, having been created from the remnants of a deep real estate recession. Increasingly, investors have turned to the conduit loan for financing, but there are some stiff requirements that can cause difficulties for the borrower.

The conduit loan is one of the great examples of America's ingenuity in regard to financial engineering. Designed to benefit the owner-developer of real estate, on the back end it also works for investors who might be looking for an alternative vehicle to park capital. Although there have been a few bumps in the road as far as development of the conduit loan process, the product has done everything (and more!) that it was designed to do.

Commercial real estate owners, developers, or investors looking to find financing for real estate turn to conduit lending in increasing numbers. By 2003, conduit loans already made up almost 20 percent of the total commercial real estate originations.[1]

Available through most major mortgage brokers, conduits are an extremely verstatile product. They can be fixed- or floating-rate; they can be offered by commercial banks, investment banks, or insurance companies; and they can be used for just about any type of structure (office buildings, industrial, hotels, apartments, self-storage, etc.).

Although fairly common now, the conduit loan was a new product just a little over a decade ago and really was developed as an outgrowth of the deep real estate recession that began at the end of 1980s. Two key things happened a bit later, in the 1990s, that planted the seeds for conduit lending. First, the federal government established the Resolution Trust Corporation as a means to deal with all the problem real estate taken from failed financial institutions. Looking to get troubled mortgages back into the public marketplace, the RTC offered pools of loans in the form of commercial mortgage-backed securities, better known as CMBS. The process was so successful that Wall Street took up the CMBS baton and in effect ran away with it. By 2004, the U.S. CMBS market reached a record $93.1 billion, almost double the amount from 1999.[2]

Also in the early 1990s, with the real estate recession in full throttle, the thrift industry collapsed and remaining lenders, from commercial banks to life insurers, scurried back from the real estate. It was tough to find financing for any project, as there was absolutely no liquidity in the marketplace. Realizing there was a void, Wall Street investment banks stepped into the commercial real estate financing breach with the conduit loan.

On a basic level, the conduit loan is simply a mortgage that is placed in a pool with other mortgages, and that large portfolio is sold to investors in the form of securities backed by those commercial mortgages.

After two decades at Lehman, Michael Mazzei moved in 2004 to Barclays Capital. His thoughts about conduits now show the benefits of the market's expansion, but also growing concerns that accompany it. "The market has become far more transparent. The risk premium associated with real estate has rightfully been reduced with the market's performance. But there is an enormous amount of competition, a lot of liquidity," he says.

NATURE OF THE BEAST

Most real estate loans such as those you might get from your local bank are considered portfolio loans in that the debt is held by the lender on its balance sheet. The conduit loan is not held by the lender; instead it is sold to investors, and that is done in a particular manner.

A conduit loan is grouped, or pooled, with other loans of varying size, property type, and location and transferred (sold) to a trust, either a real estate mortgage investment conduit (REMIC) or to a financial asset securitization investment trust (FASIT). The REMIC or FASIT segments the loans, actually issuing a series of bonds that may vary in yield, duration, and payment priority. Rating agencies such as Standard & Poor's, Fitch, and others assign credit ratings to various bond classes, ranging from investment grade (AAA/Aaa through BBB/Baa3) to below-investment-grade (BB+/Ba1) and an unrated class that is subordinate to the lowest-rated bond class.[3]

The selling of the loans is important to the borrower for the following reasons:

- The investors who buy these loans predicate their purchase on the attributes of the property (location, visibility, cash flow) rather than on the borrower or borrowing entity.

- Since conduit lenders typically look for different allocations of each asset class for a loan pool, they want diversification, which means just about any property is suitable—from retail and industrial to senior housing.[4]

- Unlike traditional loans, conduit loans are typically nonrecourse to the borrower, as they do not require personal guarantees. The reason for that is, except for cases of fraud and other unusual circumstances, the lender will look only to the property in the event of a default.[5]

As a borrower, you could probably get the most capital with a conduit loan, at a very competitive rate, and all on a nonrecourse basis.

COMPETITION BRINGS OUT THE DEALS

In the spring of 2005, conduits were still considered an excellent source of real estate financing for these reasons. The intense competition among the sources of capital was causing price undercutting, resulting in cheaper capital for borrowers. Lenders of all stripes had capital to spare, but it seemed no other group was as aggressive in getting it into the market, except for the government sponsored enterprises, or GSEs, such as Fannie Mae and Freddie Mac (they were doing so for a combination of other reasons).

One writer looking over the market early in 2005 summed it up this manner: "Borrowing money hasn't been this much fun since the late 1980s, when lenders lost the underwriting rule book and doled out capital for 110% of asset value."[6]

Leniency did abound, as it was not uncommon to be able to secure loans at 90 percent loan-to-value and very slim interest rates, sometimes as low as 70 basis points over Treasuries (interest rates on conduit loans are related to the rates paid on Treasury bonds). In less competitive times, lenders might offer an interest rate ranging from 120 to 175 basis points over the 10-year Treasury. (*Basis point* is a financing term meaning a yield of $\frac{1}{100}$ of 1 percent, and *loan-to-value* refers to the value of the loan compared to the value of the property.)

Regarding the discipline concern alluded to by Mazzei, from a consumer viewpoint conduit loans appeared "innovative and creative." While not quite so bad as offering up loans beyond asset value, underwriting terms were being bent, folded, and pounded into new shapes.

The writer who viewed the lending market as fun and innovative, turned up a fascinating deal when a real estate investment firm bought five business parks in Salt Lake City for $71 million. The investment firm wanted to be able to sell two of the business parks without a prepayment penalty. One lender's solution: financing for all five parks, but debt placed on just three. Instead of funding the five business parks with a loan-to-value of 72 percent, the lender upped the loan-to-value for the three business parks to 80 percent.[7]

Some capital sources I interviewed in the spring of 2005 were lamenting the extraordinary aggressiveness of the conduits. One fellow who headed the investment division of a large insurer noted that since the investors liked to have a mix of multifamily in any CMBS securitization, the conduits were hot to lend to that sector. The pricing was so aggressive that there was almost no spread (price above a benchmark fixed-income yield to borrow money), which meant the insurer wasn't very interested in lending to that market.

Looking over the lending situation in regard to apartment refinancing, Todd Rodenberg, senior vice president and agency director for KeyBank Real Estate Capital, a unit of KeyBank Corp., told me the market looked like a "three-ring circus," with the three rings being Fannie, Freddie, and CMBS.

In regard to multifamily business, conduit lenders in recent years have really gone after this business, which means they often go head-to-head with the GSEs. They do have some advantages over a Fannie Mae or Freddie Mac deal: (1) The main strength of the conduit loan program remains lending for the purchase or refinancing of older Class B properties; (2) conduits can beat the GSEs on new projects because the conduits can recognize value that the GSE underwriters can't (new properties have no history, an important factor for GSE financing); and (3) when combined with mezzanine financing, conduit loans can cover 90 percent, or even 95 percent, of the value of the property.[8]

One Texas business reporter wrote: "If you are pursuing a permanent loan and looking for the maximum loan proceeds and lowest interest rate, look for a conduit—chances are you'll get the best terms. Conduit lenders . . . want to get as much money out the door as quickly as possible, and they'll look at just about anything."[9]

LIMITATIONS

When opting for a conduit loan, you should carefully consider the limitations involved with such a program.

First, you need to see whether your requirements meet those of the conduit lender. In particular, conduit lending is mostly for large loans, although by 2005 a number of capital sources began offering smaller loans in the $1.5 million to $3 million range. One could probably find a conduit loan for as low as $750,000, but below that it's unlikely.

Getting through the conduit loan process is not always a fun experience, as conduits require a significant amount of data, and not just about the property. The lender can also ask for personal information. In addition, the lender might require surveys, engineering studies, deferred maintenance escrows, and vacancy escrows.[10]

Think of it this way. The underwriting standards are really set by the secondary market and as such can be very demanding, perhaps too demanding for borrowers with unique properties or borrowers who require more freedom managing their cash flow. As one online commercial lender notes, the conduit loan application process can be intimidating, because every conduit loan needs to be documented for easy sale.[11]

The trick to getting through the loan process is to be organized and stick to the set schedule. (1) Make sure historical income, expense data, rent rolls, and leases are complete, accurate, and in agreement. (2) Get personal financial statements and tax returns ready. (3) Get the lender's standard forms up front, so data can be prepared and submitted at one time. (4) Use the checklists provided by the lender. (5) Make sure all information is current, as conduit lenders cannot use information over 90 days old.[12]

Closing costs for conduit loans are generally much higher than for traditional loans, mostly because brokers charge an up-front fee to place the loan.[13] To be more competitive, the conduits are trying to be more flexible in this regard, and some lenders now charge a flat fee, minimum $10,000 to $15,000 (remember, these loans are in the multi-million-dollar range), and that would include the lender's legal fees and third-party reports.[14]

Finally, servicing (loan payments) issues can arise. Since loans are pooled and then sold, the company that made the loan is not the same as the one that is responsible for the loan after it is made, which is different from a traditional loan that is kept on the lender's books and generally serviced by that same lender.

A conduit loan can easily have three servicing agents—sub, master, and special servicer—in addition to an operating advisor (a bondholder representing the lowest ranked class of securities). As the borrower, you have no ongoing relationship with any of these groups.[15] However, a number of conduit sources are also huge servicers, so it is possible that your lender will also be your servicer.

Servicing protections do exist. All servicers and all types of servicers are defined by a pooling and servicing agreement. Although definitions may vary slightly from deal to deal, the same standard usually requires the servicer to use the same care, skill, and diligence as it uses to service and administer comparable mortgage loans.[16]

THE PREPAYMENT PROBLEM

What causes the most consternation in regard to conduit loans is the inflexibility regarding prepayments (paying off the loan prior to year span set in the contract) and any modifications.

The conduit loan is not like a traditional loan. Remember, these loans are also designed so investors could benefit at the back end by having a security that offers a set return. As noted, these loans are put into a pool with other loans; the pool is divided into levels, called *tranches,* rated by the rating agencies and sold to investors. The reason the investors are buying these securities is because they are being a promised a long-term stream of income.

The pool of mortgages serves as the underlying asset for the CMBS. When borrowers make their mortgage payment of mostly

MEET THE MAVERICKS

Michael Mazzei

Birth Date: 1961

Occupation: Managing Director and Head of Real Estate Capital Markets for Barclays Capital, New York

Education: BA, finance, Baruch College; JD, St. John's University

Career Highlights:

- Helped create the CMBS market during long stint at Lehman Brothers
- First CMBS securitization for the Resolution Trust Corp.
- Securitization of Confederation Life USA properties ignited market for non-investment-grade CMBS securities
- First wave of conduit loans to come out of Wall Street investment banks

interest and that tiny bit of principal, that money is passed through to the CMBS investors.[17]

The bondholders are investing in a security that they expect will yield a fixed interest rate over the life of the loan. As a result, the bondholders would be adversely affected by early prepayment and will normally require lockout periods and prepayment penalties to protect their investment.[18]

A typical conduit loan has a prepayment lockout for two years.

Even after the lockout is lifted, the conduit will still have serious prepayment penalties in place if the borrower opts out through defeasance (the loan is not repaid; instead, the real estate securing the loan is substituted out by other collateral, such as U.S. Treasuries).

Why do conduit lenders permit defeasance instead of allowing the loan to be repaid with penalty?

A prepayment robs the lender of interest it expects to earn over the life of the loan. And if the lender's concern is to preserve its return on investment, then a well-conceived prepayment penalty would suffice to pay the lender its anticipated return. The fly in the ointment is that the securities have competing interest about who is entitled to receive shares of the prepayment penalty. Defeasance eliminates the need to allocate the prepayment penalty among the various classes of bondholders. The lockout and defeasance provisions prevent the loan from ever being prepaid.[19]

The same inflexibility in regard to prepayment loans also exists for secondary financing. There is probably not a conduit loan that has been made that would allow additional debt to be put on a piece of real estate, whether the monies are needed to rehab or to improve the property.

Borrowers, weighing the negatives and positives, have voted with their pocketbooks in favor of the conduit loans, which are the fastest-growing category of commercial real estate loans. "More commercial real estate borrowers are diving into the opportunities offered by conduit financing. With its proven structures and acceptance by the investment community, conduit financing has created a wave of powerful results for borrowers in the form of better terms, more aggressive proceeds, and lower interest rates."[20]

Mazzei, who was lucky enough to be a young rookie in investment banking when the commercial mortgage-backed security market took its first baby steps, notes, "Wall Street has developed the technology and the transparency and built the demand for real estate capital. It began with conduit lending, but now you can go to Wall Street and get an array of capital, from the most senior interest all the way down to equity."

A LONG ROAD AHEAD

After a 20-year career with Lehman Brothers, in 2004 Michael Mazzei moved to Barclays Capital as a managing director and head of U.S. real estate capital markets. His hair was turning gray, but otherwise he had the countenance of a fellow much younger. It was a little difficult to believe he was what one person in the industry said was "one of the grandfathers" of the commercial mortgage-backed securities business.

Barclays Capital, like many investment banks, is not technically on Wall Street. The company leases offices in the MetLife Building, which sits atop Grand Central Station in the midtown area of Manhattan. When Mazzei and I sat for the interview in a conference room behind the reception desk, neither he nor I remembered that we had spoken numerous times back in the mid- to late 1990s on the subject of CMBS.

The irony was, I had only come to include Mazzei in this book on a recommendation from Tom Ferris, editor of *Commercial Mortgage Alert*, the trade publication for the CMBS industry. My original intent was to write about Ethan Penner, the flamboyant head of Nomura's CMBS unit during the first big growth wave of the business at the end of the 1990s, but he and Nomura's business crashed and burned after the credit crunch of 1998 and Penner dropped from sight.

Ferris recommended Mazzei to me, saying, "This guy has been in the business since the beginning."

Indeed he was. Back in the 1980s, there were opportunities for bright, hardworking guys from places like the Bronx. While going to college, Mazzei found a part-time job working at Merrill Lynch. After graduation and while attending law school at night, he was lucky enough to get a full-time position at what was then Lehman Brothers Kuhn Loeb. It was nothing to brag about, but it was solid work. He was doing support, essentially number-crunching for the fixed-income trading desk. Gradually, he was elevated to being an assistant at one of the mortgage trading desks.

This was back in the early 1980s when the single-family mortgage business was in an enormous growth phase and companies like Saloman Brothers and Goldman Sachs were doing great business in mortgage-backed securities—basically, bonds backed by single-family mortgages.

One of the financial pioneers early in the single-family mortgage business was a guy named Steven Sokol, who was doing work with the Federal Housing Administration (FHA) Project Loans. At first these were single-family mortgages insured by the FHA, but as the FHA's job was to inspire the construction of low-income housing it also branched into multifamily as well.

Sokol worked at Saloman Brothers and then moved to First Boston, where he started developing trading, not just in FHA project loans but also in other forms of commercial mortgage whole loans. In 1986, Sokol moved once again, this time to Lehman Brothers.

By the mid-1980s, a number of Wall Street houses were trying to come up with a way to sell commercial mortgages in a securitized way. "There were so few commercial mortgage bonds," Mazzei says with a wry smile, "we didn't even have an acronym for the stuff."

At the time, savings and loans, insurance companies, and banks were coming to Wall Street and saying, "Hey, we got these portfolios of loans. Can you slice and dice and create loan securities?"

The big problem was that the market looked, felt, and acted as if it were tabula rasa. "There was no information process, investor appetite, frequency of issuance, or rating process," Mazzei says. "You could not create homogenous pools. We didn't know what the execution could be or how to make it profitable enough for the portfolio lenders that dominated the market at the time."

At the time, single-family mortgages were being pooled and securitized, which led Wall Street to think it could also do commercial mortgages. There were just a lot more hurdles to overcome with commercial mortgages. For example, single-family mortgages were "granular," in that they were small and information you needed was slight. Plus, single-family had the support of the government through the FHA, Ginnie Mae, Fannie Mae, and Freddie Mac.

"We were all groping," recalls Mazzei. But Lehman Brothers liked the concept of commercial mortgage securitization and hired Sokol to get the ball rolling. Sokol himself was an old-school, pull-up-by-the-bootstraps kind of guy who had grown up in the Bronx, and when he began to put his team together at Lehman Brothers, he spotted a hardworking young man from outside Manhattan and, despite the fact that the man didn't have a lot of experience and didn't go to an Ivy League school, plucked him from the trading desk.

STUMBLING TOWARD EFFICIENCY

"We were struggling for years, buying and selling commercial real estate loans," says Mazzei. "Buying a loan at par and selling it up a half. It was difficult. The budget was a million dollars a month. Occasionally, something would come up where there was real estate, such as deals involving big corporate leases or CTLs."

Sometimes they got lucky, especially when a company like Wal-Mart came around. Wal-Mart then was in a big expansion mode, and Sokol could go to someone who was buying Wal-Mart stores directly because the company didn't want to own the stores and do a deal with the leases. "You could simply get levels as to where Wal-Mart bonds traded and spread the CTL story," says Mazzei. "We were looking for these kinds of pockets. We would do these kinds of esoteric deals and had enough of them to keep a small business happy."

Then came the big bang in the real estate finance business, the great real estate recession of the early 1990s, followed by the collapse of the savings and loan industry and the advent of the federal government's solution, the Resolution Trust Corp. The RTC took over failed financial institutions with the purpose of getting the troubled loans out of the government's stewardship and back into the public market.

Finally, says Mazzei, there was a seller that transcended economics. The RTC needed to get the loans out, the mortgages liquidated, the money back to the government, and find buyers. With the RTC needing to liquidate billions of dollars worth of loans, Wall Street began by securitizing the single-family mortgages. "Money was falling out of the sky, because single-family was already established and we knew how to do it efficiently," says Mazzei.

At first the RTC held onto the commercial mortgages because it didn't know what to do with them. Selling the mortgages individually would prove too inefficient, too slow.

Lehman Brothers finally discovered the formula. In 1991, it did the first securitization of commercial mortgages for the RTC, a $104 million deal involving Southern California apartment assets originated by a failed thrift, Columbia Savings and Loan of Beverly Hills, California.

"That became the model for the RTC," says Mazzei. "We bought the $104 million worth of loans on 90 Los Angeles–area multifamily properties that were auctioned off by the RTC. The loans were bought at a steep discounts due to the lack of information and the distribution risks."

At the time, there was a lot of competition for these busted mortgages, because by then a number of Wall Street firms had developed the capability of buying and selling a big portfolio of real estate. It was all good for the RTC because its goal was to sell great packages of loans to Wall Street, then watch to the see what the Street could do with the assets. In effect, the RTC was hiring the Street as agents, seeing if it could make the buying and selling programmatic.

"We bought the loans at a substantial enough discount to pay for the cost of inefficiencies," explains Mazzei. "We had to pay high fees to the rating agencies, because they were just breaking into the business and the spreads we had were actually coupons where the interest on the bonds was very high because not many investors were yet ready to buy these things."

The discount Lehman received from the government was basically a subsidy for the inefficiencies it had to pay for breaking through the market and doing the deal. In the end, Lehman sold everything in the portfolio. The RTC was so pleased that when, in 1991, it decided to do its first securitization, Lehman became the lead manager of the deal. The next year, the RTC brought another package of commercial loans to market, again with Lehman Brothers as the lead manager. That portfolio included not just multifamily, but mortgage for other assets such as office buildings.

"The RTC never started liquidating whole loans to the Street like they did with single-family loans," says Mazzei. "It almost immediately embarked on a securitization program for commercial real estate whole loan assets."

After dozens of such deals, the rating agencies became familiar with the credit support levels required to get certain ratings, and the premiums on these securitizations started to come down. Trading desks at Wall Street firms began developing a secondary market on the bonds. The RTC had proven to be the shot in the arm for the industry to grow.

GO BIG

If there was a second momentous lift for the CMBS industry, it occurred in 1996, with the denouement of Confederation Life USA, a subsidiary of Confederation Life Canada, an insurance company seized by Canadian regulators.

In 1997, Mazzei told me: "After looking at all the assets in the USA subsidiary they decided that rather than selling the asset along with the liabilities of the company as it winds down, they would sell the assets and liabilities separately. They decided to take the CMBS route."[21]

Confederation Life was a company that bet on the wrong horse at the wrong time. In order to make a profit in the increasingly competitive insurance industry, the company invested heavily in real estate throughout the 1980s and early 1990s. By 1993, 71 percent of the company's assets were in real estate. It's mortgage portfolio grew from $1.2 billion in 1982 to $8.5 billion in 1993, just in time for the great real estate recession.[22]

Two things made the deal noteworthy at the time. First, the size. It was a $1.9 billion dollar transaction. Lehman, which was the largest CMBS issuer at the time, could boast at the beginning of 1997 having done 50 transactions totaling $12 billion, of which $6 billion came in 1996, the year of Confederation Life deal.[23]

Second, the transaction was the first to test the non-investment-grade market of CMBS securities in a big way. The investment-grade portion of the deal was close to $1.6 billion, which left more than $300 million in non-investment-grade securities.

the largest non-investment-grade CMBS transaction ever offered up to that time and included five classes, starting at BB and going through nonrated.

When I talked with Mazzei in 1997, he called the deal a huge success that "catapulted the CMBS market to a new level." Recalling the transaction in 2005, Mazzei says, "Goldman Sachs was brought in as colead and we had about $15 billion in orders. It was 10 times oversubscribed. The demand that emerged for the product was very impressive."

NEXT STEP AND MISSTEP

It wasn't Lehman that took the next step—getting its own loans into the market for securitization. Mazzei gives credit to many Wall Street firms, including those no longer around (e.g., Donaldson, Lufkin & Jenrette, which began with multifamily loans—again, apartment economics seemed to be the easiest for everyone to understand). In the years 1995 through 1997, other Wall Street firms followed. "We had the infrastructure to securitize somebody else's loans and we knew the market had a demand for the product," says Mazzei. "We no longer wanted to wait for somebody else, we needed to get the product and originate it ourselves."

The mid-1990s gave rise to the conduit loans that are so ubiquitous in the market today. But growth wasn't without some serious headwinds, the most turbulent being the Russian debt crisis and collapse of hedge fund Long-Term Capital Management in 1998.

The following year, I wrote in *National Real Estate Investor,* there had been a global flight from financial risk, and "The mad rush to dump almost any kind of risk investment brought down even the high-flying CMBS market." There were a number of casualties, particularly among a pool of lesser players, WMF Group (sold to Prudential Financial), Nomura Securities (dropped out of the CMBS business), and AMRESCO (folded its tent).[24]

"Other firms pulled back in a lot of ways," Mazzei adds.

Still, even a financial crisis couldn't keep a good product down. Says Mazzei, "When 1999 came around, everyone dusted themselves off, realized it was a short-term issue, and came back full throttle. After the millennium, with the collapse of the stock market and the corporate scandals, investors turned to real estate, flocking to real estate investment trust stocks, CMBS, and other 'hard asset' classes."

Looking back after two decades, which encompassed the growth of CMBS and the emergence of the conduit loan, Mazzei told me, "That's a history of the market and my professional history as well. You can't re-create those careers."

He adds, "The market was developing, the money was coming in. It was a case of 'if you build it they will come.' "

A TRUE MAVERICK'S APPROACH TO CONDUIT LOANS

1. Shop around. A competitive market brings down the cost of loans.
2. Conduit lenders can be creative to meet your finance needs.
3. A conduit loan can be cheaper than Fannie Mae or Freddie Mac financing.
4. Conduit deals, in combination with other financings, can cover 90 percent or more of finance costs.
5. Conduit loans generally don't come in small amounts.
6. The process is difficult, so start early and be thorough.
7. A lot of data is needed just to apply for a conduit loan.
8. Closing costs can be expensive.
9. Servicer of loan may not be the company that issued the loan.
10. Conduit loans are quite inflexible in regard to prepayment.

CHAPTER 4

Agency Loans: An Easy Way to Finance Multifamily

Although Fannie Mae and Freddie Mac have been in the news quite a bit recently, this doesn't diminish what they do best, provide financing for affordable housing. Fortunately for developers, that mandate includes multifamily developments. Throw in FHA loans and there's a wide spectrum of specialized financing for apartment communities of one type or another.

David Twardock, president of Prudential Mortgage Capital Company, wasn't on my original list of real estate finance mavericks. As I was first outlining the book, I was looking for entrepreneurs. Twardock spent most of his professional career at a large company, Prudential Financial Inc., one of the largest life insurers in the United States. What I had failed to see until I began working on another article was that Twardock fell into a class even more esteemed than entrepreneur. He was a visionary who helped change the face of the real estate finance industry.

Up until the current decade, if you wanted to borrow money for a commercial real estate project, you could go to any number of sources (bank, mortgage bank, conduit, insurer, etc.) for a particular type of loan. Twardock, however, believed his company would be better able to retain customers if it could offer many different types of loans—in other words, if he could transform Prudential Mortgage Capital into a supermarket of commercial real estate financing. If a developer came to him with a project that needed an insurer-based conduit loan, Prudential Mortgage would be able to do it. A year later, if that same developer came to him once more with a project that screamed for a Fannie Mae loan, well, Prudential Mortgage could do that as well.

In 2000, when a publicly traded firm called WMF Group Ltd. slumped due to an international credit crisis, Twardock found the opportunity he needed to put his vision in place. He bought the struggling mortgage finance company, which was then the nation's largest originator of multifamily loans insured by Fannie Mae and Federal Housing Authority (FHA).

Overnight, Prudential was able to lend to commercial real estate interests through a much wider platform, and that has since become the model for a good part of the industry today. A look at

Prudential's menu of loans includes capital markets lending, life company/portfolio lending, Fannie Mae loans, FHA-insured loans, structured financing, mezzanine financing, interim/bridge lending, affordable housing loans, and forward commitments.

While all that looks good, the key for Prudential was the acquisition of the Fannie Mae and FHA platforms, which along with Freddie Mac dominate the multifamily finance sector. And that's extremely important because multifamily remains today the biggest piece of the wider commercial mortgage finance industry. In 2004, just under 40 percent of all commercial real estate loans were for multifamily developments, and that was far ahead of the second-place asset class, *office,* for which the loan origination numbers totaled about 25 percent of all commercial loans.

When one parses multifamily, for the low- and moderate-income parts of the business (where most of the lending takes place), "agencies" Fannie Mae and Freddie Mac account for more than 50 percent of the real estate financing.

Twardock realized in creating his vision that there was a crying need to be in the "agency" side of the lending business. For you, the developer, it's just possible that a multifamily project is your future, which would mean dealing with an agency loan. To make your vision happen it's important to understand the workings of and differences between the various loans.

THE FANNIE MAE APPROACH

As the largest, private-sector provider of multifamily financing, Fannie Mae operates in most sectors of affordable- and market-rate rental housing. It lends nationally, in all multifamily markets and under all economic conditions. Although the company has had structural and legislative problems of late, it still delivers more than $30 billion of multifamily financing annually.

Under its corporate charter, Fannie Mae cannot originate loans directly to borrowers, so it works through a nationwide network of correspondents called Delegated Underwriting and Servicing (DUS) lenders that have been approved to underwrite and make mortgage loans. The correspondents, which number 26, don't hold the loans, but instead sell them to Fannie Mae, which must purchase them under the DUS Agreement.[1]

By acquiring the loans, Fannie Mae puts capital back into the industry, thus providing liquidity to the mortgage banking system. The loans, however, must satisfy Fannie Mae requirements, including provisions concerning the organizational features of the borrower entities.[2] Before seeking a Fannie Mae loan, it's important to check the criteria as listed in the *DUS Guide,* sometimes known by its formal title, *Fannie Mae Delegated Underwriting and Servicing Guide.*

Here are some of the criteria for getting a Fannie Mae loan: (1) Borrower must be a U.S.-based entity directly owned by its domestic principals; (2) a limited partnership or limited liability company must be validly formed in its state of organization as per local regulations; (3) the organizational documents of the borrower must be, in the DUS lender's view, acceptable and suitable for owning and managing; and (4) the prior experience and credit reports of the borrower entity, partners, and principals need to be deemed satisfactory.[3]

Underwriting guidelines for a Fannie Mae loan include specific occupancy rate, loan-to-value and debt service criteria, and due diligence examinations (property condition, property valuation reviews, and quality of property management).[4]

All this is important because Fannie Mae doesn't decide whether the borrower is acceptable for a loan. It leaves validation and acceptance to the correspondents. However, the DUS lender is not going to be tossing out dollars willy-nilly, because it must guarantee a portion of each loan. When you have to cover, at minimum, the first

5 percent of the loan amount in the event of a default, you will be very careful about the money you are lending.

FANNIE MAE DOLLARS

Fannie Mae provides financing for acquisition, refinance, and rehabilitation of multifamily properties—all this through the DUS lender network. In addition to conventional DUS mortgage products, DUS lenders may offer financing for seniors, students, and manufactured housing. The lender can be very flexible in regard to loan terms, offering fixed-rate loans, variable-rate alternatives, interest-only adjustable-rate mortgages (ARMs), convertible ARMs, structured ARMs, and discount mortgage-backed securities (MBS).

The following are examples of some of the rate options:

- *Fixed rate.* Provide a predictable payment and amortization schedule.

- *DUS ARMs.* Variable-rate financing, choice of underlying indices, lifetime interest rate cap, and option to convert to fixed-rate loan.

- *Structured ARMs.* Competitive short-term interest rates and simple execution for single-asset loan of a minimum $25 million.

- *Discount MBS.* Short-term discount securities used to fund acquisition or refinancing.

A good thing about a Fannie Mae loan is that there is no maximum on the loan amount. Single-asset DUS loans have been known to exceed $150 million. In addition, terms are flexible, anything from 5 years to 30 years.

Here's how one DUS lender advertises its products: flexible

financing terms (interest-only, balloon, fully amortized), fixed or adjustable rates, ability to go to Wall Street pricing for individual transactions, cash or MBS pricing, special underwriting and pricing terms, interest rate buy-downs, ARM products, and credit enhancements. The loan size equal to or less than $3 million.[5] Sounds appealing enough doesn't it?

Here's how some loans played out. In May 2005, Red Mortgage Capital Inc. funded an $11,571,900 Fannie Mae MBS/DUS loan for a Section 8–assisted, age-restricted seniors housing property located north of downtown Chicago. The loan was structured as a fixed-rate loan and fully amortized over a 30-year term. As part of the refinancing, the owner was able to streamline pervious financings by extinguishing an outstanding series of bonds and paying off a mezzanine loan.[6]

To show how flexible the Fannie Mae loan can be, compare the Red Mortgage deal with this June 24, 2004, transaction by American Property Financing. Its $170 million Fannie Mae DUS loan for the refinancing of West End Towers in New York was the largest single-project DUS loan transaction in Fannie Mae's history at that time. The underwriting used $135 million in tax-exempt New York City Housing Development Corp. bonds combined with a $35 million conventional second mortgage. The entire plan fully amortizes on a 30-year schedule.[7]

Prudential Mortgage Capital has been active in Fannie Mae as well. In the first quarter of 2005 it did a $26.1 million acquisition loan for a 450-unit apartment complex in Maryland (nine-year, Fannie Mae DUS, fixed-to-floating-rate loan, amortizes over 30 years); a $12.6 million acquisition loan for a 400-unit apartment in Florida (five-year loan is interest-only through the term); and a $5.5 million refinancing loan for a 264-unit apartment complex in Texas (nine-year, DUS, fixed-to-floating-rate loan, amortizes over 30 years).

FREDDIE MAC, A DIFFERENT BEAST

For Prudential Mortgage Capital to boast a full menu of loan types, it would probably need to be a Freddie Mac Program Plus lender as well. It's a product Twardock would like Prudential to have, but so far he has not considered acquiring a company in the current Program Plus network, which consists of just 34 licensees.

Freddie Mac (originally the Federal Home Loan Mortgage Corporation) was chartered in 1970. As part of its objective, the company purchases multifamily mortgages from approved lenders in exchange for cash or multifamily, mortgage-related securities. In addition to statutory requirements for the purchase of multifamily mortgages, the company has established standards in regard to credit, appraisal, and underwriting. Guidelines are set forth in Freddie Mac's internal credit policies and in the *Multifamily Seller/Servicer Guide.*[8]

"Fannie Mae and Freddie Mac have a HUD mission—affordable housing," reiterates Twardock. "It's part of their charter. The two have financing objectives, and they have to meet and use multifamily to do that (most multifamily qualifies for Fannie and Freddie financing). As a result, they have become very important to the multifamily finance industry. They both compete on good terms, but there are differences."

Here's where the two government-sponsored enterprises align: Both adhere to the 90/90 rule, meaning the agencies want a property stabilized to the extent of having 90 percent occupancy for 90 days prior to funding; typical maximum loan-to-value is 80 percent; debt service coverage; and terms are five years to 30 years with 30-year amortizations.[9]

The three biggest differences between the two government-sponsored enterprises (GSEs) are regionalization, delegating responsibility, and risk-based pricing.

While they both use a network of correspondents, Fannie Mae's DUS lenders operate nationally, but Program Plus lenders receive state and regional authority from Freddie Mac. Second, Freddie Mac does not delegate underwriting responsibilities but reviews and approves individual loans. Third, both agencies offer risk-based pricing programs for loan requests above and below 80 percent loan-to-value, but Fannie Mae uses a tier system and Freddie Mac runs a linear program model for pricing.[10]

As a lender, one important issue for both agencies is the prepayment penalty (a charge may be imposed in the early years of a mortgage if the borrower repays the mortgage in full or pays large sums to reduce the unpaid balance).

For example, at Fannie Mae, on its traditional, 10-year, DUS MBS loan, it's possible to prepay, but with yield maintenance (a kind of prepayment deterrent fee). Partial prepayments are not allowed under any DUS MBS structure.[11]

At Freddie Mac, any prepayment of a multifamily mortgage purchased for cash or in exchange for PCs (securitization of purchased mortgages) may be subject to a prepayment premium, which can be in the form of a yield maintenance fee based on a benchmark interest rate at the time of the prepayment or on a percentage of the amount prepaid.[12]

NOD TO FREDDIE MAC

Freddie Mac lists four main advantages to its conventional mortgage program:

1. It is in the market every day and committed to offering competitive, market-driven pricing.

2. It purchases multifamily mortgages with terms from 5 to 30 years, but can customize a loan with nonstandard terms and nonstandard yield maintenance period.
3. Multifamily mortgages eligible for purchases include interest-only and fully amortizing fixed-rate mortgages, fixed-to-floating mortgages, and rate-reset mortgages (an option to extend the term at a reset interest rate).
4. It uses an early rate lock so you can lock in interest rates, establish a mortgage amount, and set out other key provisions of a proposed mortgage after a preliminary underwriting review.

Standard Mortgage Corp., a Freddie Mac Program Plus lender, used to market these features: flexible, competitive pricing options; variable loan terms; orderly, straightforward closing process; and nonrecourse and replacement reserves waived on a case-by-case basis.[13]

In February 2005, Johnson Capital Partners of Arizona, based in Phoenix, provided $4,960,000 in financing for a 126-unit apartment complex in Mesa, Arizona. The deal was done under Johnson Capital's Freddie Mac loan program. The loan was closed in 60 days at 80 percent of purchase price and a start rate of 3.70 percent.[14]

FHA BUSINESS

The aforementioned loan and the Fannie Mae loan transacted by American Property Financing (discussed earlier) doesn't look too much different from this loan: a $6 million refinancing for a 240-apartment complex in Galveston, Texas. The FHA loan amortizes over 30 years. D. Ansley Company originated the loan as a correspondent to Prudential Mortgage Capital.

Prudential Mortgage boasts a singular unit, Prudential Huntoon

Paige, which deals with FHA lending. It's one of the largest FHA multifamily lenders in the nation, originating and servicing long-term, fully amortized, fixed-rate, nonrecourse loans from origination offices located throughout the country. Part of the reason for a division that deals solely with the FHA is that these loans can be difficult, or as Prudential notes, "tricky," and it's important to have a specialist doing the deals.

The Federal Housing Administration was created under the National Housing Act of 1934. Its original concept was to attract private- and public-sector credit into the housing market to meet mortgage financing needs of low- and moderate-income multifamily mortgages. That role hasn't changed. The FHA facilitates the construction and maintenance of multifamily housing by providing mortgage insurance to finance the construction, purchase, rehabilitation, or the refinancing of rental housing.[15] The key words here are "providing mortgage insurance." Unlike Fannie Mae and Freddie Mac, the FHA doesn't buy loans; it provides insurance.

Out of the cash flow of a property approved for FHA-insurance financing, the borrower pays a mortgage insurance premium, or MIP, to the lender, which is then passed through to FHA in return for the insurance. The MIP charged is intended to compensate FHA for its risk and cost of doing business, including the expected cost of default.[16]

THE PROCESS

FHA-insured loans are made by third-party, private-sector lenders that have been approved for participation. Due to the innate bureaucracy of the federal program, each type of FHA mortgage loan is insured under a different provision of the National Housing Act. Nevertheless, under each of these programs, HUD insures the

MEET THE MAVERICKS

David Twardock

Birth Date: 1957

Occupation: President of Prudential Mortgage Capital Company

Education: BS, civil engineering, University of Illinois; MBA, finance and behavioral science, University of Chicago

Career Highlights:

- Successfully headed Prudential's divestiture of real estate holdings
- Oversaw expansion of Prudential Mortgage Capital
- Acquired The WMF Group
- Created the "supermarket" model for real estate lending
- Formed "power partnership" with Wells Fargo & Co., Bear Stearns & Co. Inc., and Nationwide Life Insurance Co. to securitize loans

repayment to the lender of the amounts payable under the mortgage loan. Some of the loans, known by their National Housing Act section code, have become very popular. Section 221(d)(4) and Section 223(f) are sought for the following reasons: The loan amount (on a debt-to-equity basis) can be generous; the loan is long term; interest rates can be attractive; and, except for some specific cases, the loan is nonrecourse. Once the FHA is satisfied with the organizational features of the borrower entity, HUD's formal written commitment will closely follow.[17]

Key points on an FHA loan (e.g., the 542(c) loan for multifamily housing development) as determined by one lender are as follows:

- *Term.* Not to exceed 35 years for existing property and 40 years for new construction projects.

- *Amount.* Limited to 85 percent of value for existing property or 90 percent for new construction projects.

- *Prepayment.* Limited and subject to the terms of the loan funding source.

- *Eligible borrowers.* Single-asset mortgagors, including nonprofit organizations, for-profit corporations, joint ventures, limited liability companies, and partnerships.[18]

A peek at FHA-insured loans from individual lenders shows a very competitive product. ARCS Commercial Mortgage Company LP, for example, offers five different FHA products. Here's the way it lays out some of them:

- *221(d)(3) and 221(d)(4) loans.* Provides mortgage insurance to facilitate the new construction and substantial rehabilitation of multifamily rental properties. Terms of up to 40 years, competitive fixed-interest rates, AAA credit enhancement for tax-exempt bond-financed transactions, and eligibility for securitization by Ginnie Mae. Loans are nonrecourse and allow higher loan-to-cost ratios and lower debt service coverage. Also, the loan can convert to permanent upon completion of the building phase.

- *223(f) loans.* Provides mortgage insurance for the refinance, acquisition, and moderate rehabilitation of existing multifamily rental properties. Terms of up to 35 years, fully amortizing, and no rent restrictions or affordable leasing requirements. Competitive fixed rates, AAA credit enhancement for tax-exempt bond-financed transactions, and eligibility for securitization by Ginnie Mae. Loans are nonrecourse and allow higher loan-to-value and lower debt service coverage. To qualify the structure has to be three years from the end of construction or its last substantial rehabilitation.[19]

What does one of these loans look like? In May 2005, Red Mortgage Capital Inc. closed an FHA-insured mortgage loan to finance an existing assisted living facility in Hobart, Indiana. Red Mortgage processed and funded the $4,150,000, 35-year, nonrecourse loan that was insured through FHA's Section 232/223(f) mortgage insurance program.[20]

FORMING THE MODEL

In 2004, a Cleveland-based bank, National City Corporation, acquired Provident Financial Group primarily to enter the Cincinnati market, where the latter was based, but with that acquisition came a couple of bonuses. With the deal, National City also got Capstone, a mortgage broker with a Freddie Mac license for the states of Ohio and Kentucky, and Red Capital Group, a Fannie Mae DUS lender.

Suddenly, National City became a broad-based commercial real estate lender with key multifamily financing programs. In a sense, it looks a lot like Prudential Mortgage Capital, which is not surprising since a lot of lenders have co-opted the model.

His vision for a commercial lending supermarket was not David Twardock's only real estate epiphany. His first occurred much earlier in his life—I would say "career," but when he visualized his first creative concept he didn't really have a career. What he had was a job, and it wasn't a very good one.

After growing up in Champaign, Illinois, Twardock traveled no farther than the length of a couple streets to go to college, at the University of Illinois, where he earned a degree in civil engineering. That was a good background, apparently, for his first real job, as an elevator salesman for the Otis Elevator Co. After about two years, Twardock found himself again standing on a couple of two-by-fours peering down and down and down to the bottom of the elevator pit—which was exactly where his career was going. At that moment, or one just like it, he realized that the elevator guys were not making much money. The real dough was being made by the developers who subcontracted jobs such as elevator installations.

That was Twardock's first creative breakthrough, and it wasn't necessarily correct, but he did quit his job as an elevator salesman to go to work at Prudential, which at the time was one of the largest real estate developers in the country. When Twardock joined the company, Prudential had a practice of rotating new hires through different parts of its real estate business. One of the first deals Twardock worked on was ascertaining the value of land under the Playboy building in Chicago so it could be sold. After that, Twardock managed 30 industrial buildings. Finally he moved to acquisitions.

By 1984, Twardock was everywhere but in development. He wasn't going to get any closer, because that year Prudential was going through one of its serial reorganizations, and this one would create a new mortgage division. An executive at the new unit remembered Twardock and tapped him for the mortgage start-up. "I was pissed off," Twardock recalls. "I wanted to be a developer and now I was as far from being a developer as I could get."

Despite his annoyance at the turn of events, Twardock realized he couldn't have ended up in a better spot at Prudential. His first new position was being a loan officer. "It was great because it was new ground, new people," he says. "It was not like I was buried in an organization. I was really able to step up very quickly in the new organization, and that made a difference."

If Twardock had gone over to the development end, his tenure at Prudential might have ended quicker than he would have wanted, because insurers that are publicly traded no longer own as much real estate as they once did. Mortgages, however, are another story. Typically, insurance companies do not need a lot of liquidity because most of the liabilities (insurance policies) are long term in nature and match up well with mortgages, which are also long term in nature. In addition, commercial mortgages are often locked out to prepayment or have yield-maintenance protection so that they maintain the long-term objective even in different interest rate environments.

Twardock quickly moved up the management ladder of Prudential Mortgage Capital, and in the mid-1990s he took over Prudential's general account, real estate equity group, then called Prudential Realty. At the time, Prudential was still one of the country's biggest owners of commercial real estate, but it no longer wanted to be such a big landowner.

"We were focused on getting out of the direct ownership of real estate," says Twardock. Instead, Prudential Realty was moving into ownership of operating companies, such as real estate investment trusts. After three busy and successful years, Twardock was asked in 1998 to move once again, this time to run Prudential Mortgage Capital, which is where he had been before.

Insurers lend to commercial real estate developers and owners through a network of correspondents. These mortgages produced by the correspondents are then held in portfolio. In 1997, the year before Twardock came back to Prudential Mortgage Capital, it had added a new lending vehicle to its program, a conduit. With a conduit loan, Prudential's mortgages could then be placed in a pool of loans to be securitized and sold to investors. It was a different product, with different characteristics, and gave Prudential another means to lend money.

Although Twardock liked the new product, Prudential's conduit business wasn't growing very quickly, one of the reasons being that the GSEs were expanding so aggressively, thus making it tough competition for conduits.

"We were achieving success with the conduits," says Twardock, "but we were losing business to the agencies. So I thought maybe we should be in the agency business as well. Let's go talk to Fannie Mae."

That was a big leap of faith, because there were at the time (and still are) just 26 Fannie Mae DUS lenders. For the most part, these were independent, entrepreneurial mortgage banking firms that took a gamble on the Fannie Mae multifamily business (Fannie Mae was mostly a single-family lender) when the big lenders such as commercial banks, investment banks, and insurance companies wouldn't touch the program. The sticking point for the big lenders was that to be a Fannie Mae lender, you had to take a portion of the risk on every loan (the top 5 percent of any loss, then a portion of any subsequent loss). After the great real estate recession of the late 1980s and early 1990s, lenders were looking to reduce real estate risk, not increase it.

For Twardock to even consider becoming a Fannie Mae lender was extremely radical thinking at the time, but Twardock was already envisioning the future. To be a Fannie Mae lender was just a logical extension of what Prudential Mortgage Capital was already doing with the conduit business—an attempt to commercialize and earn profits on the company's real estate lending practices.

"We recognized the market was going to become more competitive and our goal was to attract and retain relationships with borrowers," Twardock says. "In order to do that, we needed to be able to offer a selection of capital, whether it was our portfolio loan, or conduit, and after the WMF Group purchase, a Fannie Mae or FHA loan. We realized if we didn't offer a particular type of loan, someone else would."

In 1998, WMF began a conduit program (about the same time as Prudential), but when the world debt crisis hit, WMF Group (a Virginia lender) could not handle the financial fallout. The turmoil didn't bankrupt WMF, but it had to shut down the conduit, downsize, and restructure. Prudential, along with all other conduits, was smacked by the financial crisis, but Prudential was much bigger and had the financial strength to weather the storm.

One step Prudential did take was incorporating the existing conduit into the whole Prudential Mortgage Capital structure. "The conduit started out as almost a stand-alone activity for its first year," says Twardock, "but when we bought WMF, we focused on bringing all the servicing into one location, having one original platform."

By the year 2000, there was already a consolidation movement afoot in the real estate financial markets. In 1998, PNC Financial Services Group acquired Midland Loan Services, a Kansas City–based company that originated, securitized, and serviced conduit loans. However, Midland wasn't a GSE lender.

"None of the major real estate financial firms had acquired an agency lender. We were the first," says Twardock. (In 2001, one year after the WMF deal, PNC acquired TRI Capital Corporation, a Freddie Mac and FHA lender.)

"We were confident we could make it work," says Twardock. "We had already made the decision that we were going to make the transition to being a mortgage finance company. I wouldn't have taken the job as head of Prudential Mortgage Capital if I was not confident we could move in that particular direction."

Five years after the WMF deal, I'm guessing there's probably not another life insurer that has acquired an agency lender. When I asked Twardock whether that was true, he stopped for a moment before answering. It was as though he had never considered the question before. "I think that is right," he responded. Then he added, "Frankly, I'm surprised more insurance companies have not done it. That's because they are very focused on their own portfolios. If we hadn't formed our conduit the way we did and started to think of real estate lending as a business rather than as an investment, I doubt we would have made the transition."

Life insurers, which today are still major lenders to real estate, for the most part consider real estate loans as an investment. Twardock had the lending practices of Prudential formed as a separate operating subsidiary. "We capitalized it separately; we ran it as a separate profit and loss center, and with that we made the mental transition from being an investment to being a business."

While life insurers have been reluctant to follow the "supermarket" model, other lenders, particularly banks, have not. A partial list of banking and investment banking companies tracking the same route as Prudential include Wachovia Corp. (acquired Lend Lease Mortgage Capital and AMI Capital Inc.), Credit Suisse First Boston's Column Financial Inc. (Investment Property Management LLC and commercial mortgage operations of Standard Mortgage Corporation), Deutsche Bank (Berkshire Mortgage LP), and Key-Corp's Key Bank Real Estate Capital (American Capital Resources Inc., National Realty Funding, Newport Mortgage, and Conning Asset Management's real estate mortgage division).

PRUDENTIAL'S NUMBERS

In 2000, the year Prudential Mortgage Capital acquired WMF Group, it recorded what was then a record $3.5 billion in mortgage originations. By 2004, that number had grown to $8 billion. While a considerable portion of the 2004 totals, $3.5 billion, can be attributed to the company's general account (loans kept by Prudential for its own portfolio), the third-largest contributor was Fannie Mae, at $1.119 billion. FHA loans were the fifth-largest contributor at $167 million—actually a subpar year for Prudential's FHA unit, which usually produces about $400 million in loans.

In 2004, the company's median loan size ran $8.4 million, while the average loan came in at $14.1 million. The company offers loans in all sizes, from about $2 million to more than $100 million.

By asset class, the loans broke out in this manner: multifamily at 35 percent, office 21 percent, industrial 17 percent, retail 16 percent, and other (hotels, flex, healthcare, self-storage, senior housing, etc.) at 11 percent. Obviously, the multifamily was supported by the Fannie Mae and FHA lending capabilities.

When the company set its goals for 2006, it placed more emphasis on using Prudential's balance sheet to drive lending activities, particularly in its capital markets and the multifamily programs of affordable housing, Fannie Mae, and FHA.

What's interesting is that when Prudential Mortgage Capital lists loan types it singles out the Fannie Mae Revolving Credit Facilities as well as the usual permanent fixed-rate loans, floating-rate loans, interim loans, bridge loans, mezzanine loans, forward commitments, and acquisition/bridge/rehabilitation loans.

"The mortgage process is not an easy one," says Twardock. "We have done research on this, and if borrowers have had a good experience the borrowers will want to go back to where they had done business before. The reason our model works is because if we have the right source of capital on deal one, say it is a general account loan, then I should have the right source for deal two, perhaps a conduit loan. If I'm not on both loans, then the borrower will go elsewhere, start a relationship with that second company, and Prudential has lost the edge."

Twardock hasn't been in a hurry to pick up a Freddie Mac lender, mostly because they tend to lend regionally. This is not to say the company may not be offering Freddie Mac loans in the future. "From our perspective, I am trying to make sure the borrowers and brokers that I deal with can get what they need from me," he says. "If I had Freddie Mac, I would pretty much have the suite of things that I need. Currently, I'm losing some business to Freddie Mac, and I don't like to lose business. Not having Freddie Mac gives borrowers a chance to deal with someone else, and I would rather have them deal with me."

A TRUE MAVERICK'S APPROACH TO AGENCY LENDING

1. Fannie Mae loans originated through network of correspondents called Delegated Underwriting and Servicing (DUS) lenders.
2. Before seeking Fannie Mae loan, check DUS guidebook.
3. Fannie Mae provides for acquisition, refinance, and rehabilitation of multifamily projects.
4. There's no maximum on a Fannie Mae loan.
5. Fannie Mae and Freddie Mac use the 90/90 rule (90 percent occupancy for 90 days).
6. Fannie Mae and Freddie Mac loans have prepayment penalties.
7. Before seeking a Freddie Mac loan, consult its seller/servicer guidebook.
8. Freddie Mac loans are generally from 5 to 30 years, but they can be customized.
9. Freddie Mac offers an early-rate-lock provision.
10. Out of the property cash flow of FHA-approved financing, the borrower pays a mortgage insurance premium (MIP).
11. Popular FHA loans offer long-term, nonrecourse features with attractive interest rates.
12. FHA loans provide mortgage insurance to facilitate new and existing project refinancing, acquisition, and rehabilitation.

CHAPTER 5

Giving It Up for Equity Financing

If you're looking to fill in the missing piece of debt between bank loans and your own capital, you might want to consider equity financing. Third-party equity investors will want to share on the upside if everything turns out well—and that might seem at first glance prohibitive—but equity financing deals aren't onerous, and the terms become more generous the more successful the investment.

It's a brilliant, clear day in Houston and I'm sitting on the forty-fourth floor of an office tower located not in downtown but somewhere out in the burbs. This is the odd thing about Houston: These high-rise buildings constructed far from downtown stand by themselves like the last palm tree on the beach.

Since the Houston area is flat, I can see as far as the far horizon—miles into the distance. Every once in a while, I look out at the view while listening to Brian Stoffers, chief operating officer of L.J. Melody & Company, a Capital Markets division of CB Richard Ellis company. He is teaching me the value of equity financing.

Equity financing can be very confusing. It's an expensive way to finance a deal and often sits in the debt stack at about the same place as mezzanine financing, especially in complex deals where a lot of different loan structures are needed to complete a transaction.

However, Stoffers says equity financing can be cheaper than other forms of financing, and as he explains the process, I'm thinking it's not so confusing after all. Stoffers knows all this because L.J. Melody, a commercial mortgage banking firm, provides a broad array of flexible financing options, including permanent loans, construction loans, mezzanine financing, and equity transactions.

ATTAINABLE

The company is not unique. A host of mortgage banking and investment banking companies clearly boast an ability to do equity financing. Today, it's about as commonplace as a bank loan, whether it be from big or small capital sources.

Pacific Security Capital, a Beaverton, Oregon, commercial real estate bank, runs offices in Los Angeles and Florida, plus works with correspondents in Houston, Chicago, and New York. It offers a very thorough equity financing program and will consider multifamily, retail, industrial, office, hospitality, and condominium projects for the following types of investments: development, recapitalization, renovation, and yield plays. Deal size it prefers: $5 million to $50 million per property, plus it will fund up to 95 percent of the required equity amount. It likes to see sponsor contributions of between 5 and 10 percent.[1]

It's an interesting menu because, supposedly, there isn't a lot of equity finance capital available for small to midsize property owners, mostly because large institutional lenders won't consider deals below a certain threshold—and because most friends and family don't have an extra million or so lying around to invest.

Like Pacific Security Capital, another West Coast lender, Hanover Financial Company of Los Angeles, fills in what is really a midprice range of equity finance, $5 million to $30 million.[2]

Then there is the small, Long Island real estate office that boasts it is able to secure equity financing on most real estate projects. Its online advertisement claims: "Our sources of finance can respond to situations that are time, interest rate or dollar sensitive. We have access to foreign and domestic funds willing to invest equity development capital on a joint venture basis on real estate acquisition and/or development projects." Optimally, this firm will invest up to 90 percent or more of the equity required (or possibly more under exceptional circumstances). This means that if a construction or acquisition lender will do 70 percent of the costs, then the fund will capitalize up to 90 percent of the equity required, generally on a nonrecourse basis. There is no upper dollar limit or geographic restriction on projects they would consider.

FILLING IN THE CAPITAL STACK

If you as a developer find a piece of property and want to build con-dominiums, for example, then in all likelihood you will need to bor-row money for the project. You figure the cost for development will be $50 million. You have $5 million in your pocket that you will invest. However, your local bank will lend only $35 million. That leaves you $10 million short. But you can still reach that $50 million dollar amount by getting a mezzanine loan, equity financing, or combination of both.

That's the reason there is confusion, because those mezzanine dol-lars and equity financing sit in the financing stack on top of the sen-ior mortgage loan. This positioning is important only to the lenders themselves, because in the event that your project doesn't work out, the senior mortgage loan is paid off first. The mezzanine loan and/or equity financing, because they are second in line in case of default, carry higher risk and therefore will cost more.

What makes the two more confusing is that lenders will, in essence, market capital in a blended way. As an example, Legg Mason Real Estate Investors, Inc., offered what it called preferred equity financing, which it says, "can resemble a mezzanine loan and be useful when secondary financing is prohibited or can be used for transactions that require an equity partner due to risk profile or deal structure."

Another company, the Scot-Mor Group of Companies in Ontario, Canada, claims it has capital available in the form of "mez-zanine equity financing."

In most situations there is a true difference between a *mezzanine loan,* which is a form of debt, and *equity financing,* which creates an ownership position in terms of reward for the investment.

In that so-called stack of financing, the senior mortgage capital comes first, followed by the mezzanine piece, and at the tail end is all the equity investment, including your capital. The reason capital providers make the distinction is because they try to stratify the total real estate capital structure into tranches and then to match the different risk profiles associated with each tranche with the appropriate yield requirement.[3]

For the sake of argument, let's follow the c-lender "Scotsman Guide" in explaining how this plays out. I use this example because it clearly differentiates between mezzanine and equity financing and does so in this manner: Mezzanine is (1) any capital contribution to the total real estate transaction placed behind the senior mortgage loan and in front of equity; (2) the piece of the loan stack from around 75 percent of the cost of investment, property, development, and so on, to 85 or 90 percent; and (3) any capital above 90 percent is considered equity.

If the loan stack has three entities, or tranches (senior mortgage loan, mezzanine, and equity), each will have a different risk, and as a borrower you pay an increasingly higher amount for each level or risk. This meant, in the first half decade after the turn of millennium, the lender involved in the senior mortgage loan charged interest only in single digits, but the mezzanine lender charged interest in double digits, and the equity finance source requires a return in excess of the mezzanine lender. As a rule, equity investors usually require a minimum yield on the invested capital plus participation in the ownership of the real estate, chiefly in the form of sharing cash flow from operations or sharing the capital gains from the sale of the real estate.[4]

SOUNDS EXPENSIVE, BUT NOT REALLY

The equity finance end always seemed a bit pricey to me, but Stoffers suggests looking at a deal in a different manner. When borrowers capitalize a project, they either come with their own equity, get equity from friends and family, or go to a third party. Stoffers maintains the equity that an L.J. Melody arranges can be less expensive than what the borrower might arrange with family and friends. As noted in the preceding paragraph, the equity investor usually wants some participation in the return, but in 2005 there was so much capital available, fixed-income equity was available. What the equity finance investors actually got was a fixed, preferred return with prospects of being able to share in the profits thereafter.

"As a developer you might have the $10 million that can be entirely used to do a $10 million development," Stoffers explains. "But you might just put up $2 million and save the other $8 million for four other projects. A mortgage banker will come up with the other $8 million. You are putting up less of your own capital, but are contributing your development expertise and knowledge. By leveraging (borrowing), you can place your bets on four deals rather than one."

The founder of Hanover Financial, Mark Macedo, observed, "Many developers over time have been stuck doing one project a year, when really, they have the capacity to do four or five projects in a year."[5]

How does this work? Here's an older deal clearly defined. L.J. Melody arranged $26 million in construction and equity financing for a 360-unit apartment complex to be built in Fort Myers, Florida. First Union National Bank provided the construction financing, and Nationwide Realty Investors provided equity financing.[6]

GOOD FINANCING FOR APARTMENTS, BUT CAN BE USED ALMOST ANYWHERE

Equity finance is very popular in regard to the capitalization of apartment communities. Over the course of a few months at the end

MEET THE MAVERICKS

Brian Stoffers

Birth Date: 1958

Occupation: Chief Operating Officer, Executive Managing Director of L.J. Melody Company, a CB Richard Ellis company; President of CB Richard Ellis Capital Markets

Education: BA, accounting, California State University at Fullerton; MBA, San Diego State University

Career Highlights:

* Helped merge CB Richard Ellis takeover L.J. Melody Company
* Joint venture with GE Capital to form mortgage servicing giant, GEMSA Loan Services LP
* Company has become one of the top two mortgage originators in the country
* Acquired Insignia/ESG

of 2004 and beginning of 2005, Franklin Capital Group (or its subsidiary Franklin Capital Advisors LP) of Alexandria, Virginia, announced, among many other deals, the following: $3.5 million equity financing of the 64-unit Azalea Park Apartments in Summerville, South Carolina; the acquisition, rehabilitation, and equity financing of Village Green Apartments in Bowling Green, Kentucky; $6.8 million equity financing of Marina Del Ray Apartments in Beverly Hills, California; $4.3 million equity financing of The Lakes Apartments in Nashville; and the equity financing of three rental properties in Culpeper, Fredricksburg, and Leesbury, Virginia.[7]

By no means does this mean equity finance is limited to multi-family; it can be used for almost any asset class. In a deal from 2004, the Sonnenblick-Eichner Company of Los Angeles arranged land acquisition and joint venture equity financing for the proposed $130 million Viceroy Anguilla Resort & Residences, located on the island of Anguilla in the Caribbean. In an earlier deal, Kennedy Wilson of Beverly Hills, California, arranged the equity financing for the acquisition of 370 Lexington Avenue in New York, a 27-story office building.[8]

"There is so much money out there today that equity finance sources feel they are getting well compensated for their risk by coming into a position where they won't get all the upside, but a nice return instead," says Stoffers.

Looking back at his $10 million deal, let's see what Stoffers is talking about. Remember, we mentioned the source of capital may want a fixed, preferred return (upon sale or refinance, the investor is investment paid back, along with the required return, before the developer). If the deal is for the $8 million, then the investor might want a preferred return of 10 percent. That means the equity finance partner will get $800,000 a year until paid off. Does that seem like a lot? It isn't when you consider that as the developer you are putting up only $2 million, whereas your equity partner is putting up $8 million.

PROMOTES AND PERCENTAGES

If the returns go to 12 percent, then in this deal the extra return is split on a percentage basis, 80 percent to 20 percent (the same as the capital infusion percentage). However, when the property is sold, the internal rate of return turns out to be 15 percent. The difference between that number and 12 percent is more than the equity finance partner expected, so instead of splitting 80-20 for the bonus, that partner will give the entrepreneur a split of 70-30 or even 60-40. Why? Because the entrepreneur is being rewarded for his or her intelligence, leadership, leasing capabilities, ability to come in under budget, and any number of other things. "From the borrower's perspective, rather than sharing equally, now you can get a return that is not equal to your partners; you are getting a *promote*," says Stoffers.

The proceeds split 80-20 until both parties receive their principal back plus a set return (as the preferred party, the investor is paid back first), after which the developer could be "promoted" up to 30 percent of the remaining cash flow. After the required preferred return is satisfied, proceeds are generally split according to a predetermined "waterfall" of return hurdles and splits. (The waterfall can be complex or very simple, with only one or two levels, or promotes.[9]

That's the way these things work, Stoffers adds. "Between 12 and 15 percent, the entrepreneur gets 30 percent of the deal. Maybe between 15 and 20 percent, the entrepreneur gets 40 percent. If the project is a grand slam and it makes a ton of money, your equity partners will be very happy, because they have an increasing share without taking the risks you did and without the sweat equity. They are willing to let you end up with a 30 percent return, and that is why you bring in third-party money."

A common equity structure is for the equity finance investor to provide 80 to 90 percent of the equity gap, which is amount of capital required, after senior debt financing and your own capital, to reach the cost of the investment.

If the senior loan goes to 75 percent, for example, then the equity gap would be the remaining 25 percent of cost. If the third-party equity financier provides 80 percent of the equity gap (80 percent of 25 percent is 20 percent), then the developer will pony up the remaining 5 percent. Using that split on a $20 million transaction would mean a $15 million first-mortgage loan, a $4 million third-party equity investment, and a $1 million developer equity investment.[10]

As noted, a common equity financing structure is up to 90 percent of the equity gap; however, over the past couple of years equity financing has loosened up. Earlier I mentioned a company called Pacific Security Capital. It will fund up to 95 percent of the required equity amount. It likes to see the developer contribute between 5 and 10 percent. Its preferred return is in the 8 to 12 percent range plus tiered returns (ownership percentages based on mutually established hurdle rates and benchmarks designed to affect the target returns).[11]

The company called Scot-Mor that was offering the mezzanine equity financing for acquisitions or construction made this notation: "By utilizing creative financial structures, a developer can contribute, say, 20% (or less in some cases) of the project's equity requirement and yet realize 50% of the project's net profits [a generous deal, as it is very rare to go to 50 percent and even rarer to go beyond]. In that situation where a developer has obtained significant pre-leasing for a new development, in certain cases, Scot-Mor can arrange financing for 100% of the project's cost! . . . In general terms, development profits are split 50-50 between the developer and equity financier. The 100% financing is provided to the developer on a nonrecourse basis in the form of a joint venture structure."[12]

CREATING COMPANIES THAT FINANCE DEVELOPMENT

Lawrence J. Melody tells me he doesn't think too much about mortgages anymore. He's too involved in his golf game. "Lately," he says, "they just drag me out to play golf with potential customers."

Melody deserves a little leisure time now and then, because he worked for 40 years in the commercial mortgage industry and founded two major companies, both of which are still active, major competitors in the mortgage banking industry. Dallas-based L.J. Melody Co., the firm that bears his name, is now part of the CB Richard Ellis, and the first company he created, Northmarq Capital Inc., operates out of Minneapolis and is now part of Marquette Financial Companies.

Back around 1960, there were a lot of things going on in Lawrence Melody's life. He attended Columbia Law School for a year, but when he got married he lost his scholarship. He left law school and moved to Hartford, Connecticut, where he got a job with Connecticut General Corporation (now Cigna Corporation). "I was lucky to get the job, because I was eligible for the draft, and no one was hiring anybody who had not completed their draft status," Melody recalls.

He got lucky once again when his wife found out she was pregnant, which gave Melody a "father's exemption" from serving in the military. "That was the last I ever heard from the military," he says now, still with visible relief.

Connecticut General was one of the four or five major life insurers doing commercial loans at the time; most of the other insurers were investing in residential mortgages. The insurers liked—and still do—real estate because as an investment it matches up well with liabilities.

There were only about six guys in the Connecticut General commercial department then, and they did it all. There was no legal or closing staff, but there were national accounts. Connecticut General worked with correspondents around the country. Melody's territory was the Southeast and Southwest, two fast-growing areas. At that time, a $5 million loan was huge. Now the average loan size at L.J. Melody stands at $13.5 million.

MEET THE MAVERICKS

Lawrence Melody

Birth Date: 1937

Occupation: Founder, Chairman of the L.J. Melody Company, a CB Richard Ellis company

Education: BA, political science, Notre Dame University

Career Highlights:

- Founded Northland Mortgage, now Northmarq Capital
- Founded L.J. Melody Company
- Transformed L.J. Melody into a national mortgage banking concern
- Merged L.J. Melody Company into CB Richard Ellis

FIRST START-UP

Melody's father worked in the single-family residential business. After growing up in Midwest, his father took a job back east with Lomas & Nettleton Mortgage Company, the first residential mortgage company to reach $1 billion in servicing. But Melody's father's heart was in the Midwest, and he changed employers, taking a job running the mortgage company for the family of Hamm's Brewing Company. The first thing he did was talk his son into coming along and starting a commercial loan operation, which became Northland Mortgage, now Northmarq Capital.

Melody had worked at Connecticut General until 1967, when he left to form Northland, but he was so highly thought of at his old company that Northland became a correspondent for Connecticut General. "They gave me that account right after I moved out there," says Melody. "Our expansion plans were to grow our company around Connecticut General and Metropolitan Life. At that time, if you had those two accounts you almost didn't need any other accounts."

Around 1976, Melody's life again entered the vortex. After his father retired, he got a call from his old company, now Cigna. He was still so well regarded there that when Cigna decided to make a change with its correspondents in Texas, the company called Melody looking to make a deal. Since he used to handle that territory, would he like to start a company there to be Cigna's correspondent? It seemed like a good idea. Instead of owning a small portion of Northland, he could create his own company.

In 1976, L.J. Melody Company was formed, 80 percent owned by Lawrence Melody and 20 percent owned by John Bradley, who had worked with Melody at Northland. Actually, it wasn't as simple as Melody makes it sound. The new company had a lender source, but no capital sources. So the new firm paid $500,000 to buy the servicing of Cigna accounts that were already in Texas. It took Melody and Bradley's life savings, plus a loan from Texas Commerce Bank.

The deal that put the company on the map in Texas was actually a refinancing of an old deal done when Melody worked at Connecticut General: the building of the landmark Galleria Mall in Houston. Around 1969, The Hines Co., which built the mall, asked Melody to recapitalize its entire debt load. Melody got it done.

"It was a complicated deal where all the original lenders had to be recast, and the new debt had less controls because the original debts had been limiting the mall's ability to expand," Melody says.

Other major financings include Trump Palace Condominiums in Florida; Scottsdale Princess Resort, Arizona; 1200 Avenue of the

Americas, New York; Bethesda Place, Maryland; and Memorial City Mall, Texas.

Melody gets up from his comfy chair and looks out the window, where Houston is spread from one end of the horizon to the other. He points off to the northwest. "See that group of structures over there, the four buildings and the hotel beyond? The low white one is the hotel." The buildings he wanted me to notice were the River Way office complex, which his company had refinanced for $82 million.

L.J. Melody & Co. had been doing such a good job for Cigna that when the insurer became unhappy with correspondents in other markets, it would offer Melody those territories as well. As a result, just a few years after opening its office in Texas, L.J. Melody boasted offices in Denver, Phoenix, Los Angeles, San Diego, and Orange County, California.

The diversification worked out well for Melody because in the early 1980s the Texas real estate market began to tank.

When the Texas market collapsed, it was the first downturn Lawrence Melody experienced in his career. "We were worried about meeting our payroll," he remembers. "It was very serious. In January I knew what our total overhead was going to be for the year and I knew what our servicing income was going to be and it didn't match up. I knew we had to do a bunch of new business to stay alive." It was business Melody could do because he was operating in other markets that were nowhere near as scary as Texas was at that moment.

"We would have been dead had we not been in some other market areas," Melody says. "Also, being in those other markets gave us a chance to expand our business to include pension advisory work rather than just mortgage banking for insurance companies."

With the new source of capital, L.J. Melody was working deals all over the country. Rates were so high then, however, that most of that business was equity financing, joint ventures, or participating debt.

At about the same time, L.J. Melody established a relationship with GE Capital, and in 2001 their joint venture developed into the creation of GEMSA Loan Services LP.

In 2004, GEMSA serviced 8,000 loans valued at more than $62 billion. (Loan servicing is the management of required payments on the lender's or borrower's behalf.) GEMSA ranked as the country's fourth-largest loan servicer and the only one in the top 10 that is not owned by a bank.

As Lawrence Melody was building up his own mortgage banking company, a young Southern California man was entering the real estate business for the first time. Brian Stoffers had put himself through California State University at Fullerton working in a grocery store. He also bought and sold a couple of homes, and the taste of the real estate business turned his head away from accounting, the field in which he earned his degree. He worked briefly for a commercial brokerage operation, then dropped out to backpack around Europe before returning to San Diego, where he joined the intern program at what was then Coldwell Banker Commercial. The year was 1981.

By the following year, Stoffers ended up in CB Commercial's mortgage banking division, which oddly enough was also doing a lot of business for an insurance company, this one being Aetna Life Insurance Co. After a great deal of success in San Diego, Stoffers moved up the corporate ladder and earned his MBA from San Diego State University.

L.J. MELODY MEETS CB RICHARD ELLIS

Early in 1996, Stoffers picked up his office telephone. On the other end of the line was James Didion, chairman of CB Richard Ellis.

Didion was an interesting fellow. His sister, Joan Didion, is the accomplished author (*Play It As It Lays, Book of Common Prayer*) and screenwriter (*A Star Is Born, Panic in Needle Park*). People say James Didion is just as brilliant in business as his sister is in literature.

"You met with Jim, and I did an article about the two of us," Melody reminded me. I didn't remember it. I recall visiting with Gary Beban, who was then president of CB Commercial. Beban was also an interesting guy, having been a Heisman Trophy–winning quarterback at UCLA and for a short period of time a Washington Redskin. CB Commercial had unique personalities back then.

Anyway, Didion had struck up a conversation with Lawrence Melody at a recent conference and wanted Stoffers to go out to Houston to meet with him. The result was the acquisition of the L.J. Melody Co. by CB Richard Ellis.

One of the things that caught the eye of Didion was that in 1996, L.J. Melody was already one of the top mortgage servicers in the country, with $3.5 billion under management (compared with the $62 billion in servicing today!).

"The situation with our own company was that the West Coast of the mortgage banking platform was doing quite well, but east of the Rockies we were struggling," says Stoffers. "Larry Melody, with his home base in Texas, really had come to dominate there and in places like Denver. He had offices in California, but they were smaller. Our businesses were complementary, and what we could do for him was give him the ability to grow."

Melody doesn't even blink twice when the subject of the sale of his company comes up. Even today, he thinks it was the right thing to do. "They had a mortgage banking operation that was about the same size as mine," he says. "We were doing $3.5 billion in servicing; they were about $3 billion. We had six offices; they had 25.

They were really national, with offices where they also had broker-age and lease activities. They were not making any money, and Jim liked to make money. We were making money, but had some limi-tation on expansion potential. The fit turned out to be pretty good."

After the two mortgage banking operations merged, L.J. Melody, a CB Richard Ellis operation, made eight more acquisitions, filling in the rest of the country with premium mortgage banking firms. In 1998, its busiest year, it acquired Cauble & Company of Carolina, in Charlotte; North Coast Mortgage Company, Seattle and Port-land; Shoptaw James Inc., Atlanta and Tampa; and Carey Brum-baugh Starman & Philips, Pittsburgh.

In one of its biggest deals in 2002, L.J. Melody acquired Insignia/ESG, of Washington, D.C.

"We think we acquired some of the best companies across the country from 1997 to 2002," Stoffer notes. "The key for us has been the ability to integrate them into the overall platform and make them hum. In fact, the sum of the parts is greater than the individ-ual pieces. They are doing more business with lenders than they ever have, and business continues to grow."

This isn't to say L.J. Melody no longer pioneers a new market. Between 2002 and 2004 it opened offices in Philadelphia, Tucson, Baltimore, and Toronto, Canada. Today the company runs 35 offices. The firm presently has a team in London looking for some initiatives in the United Kingdom. L.J. Melody is also mulling a future representation in the Far East.

In 2004, L.J. Melody originated $13.3 billion in transactions, making it the second-largest originator that year. Another entre-preneurial firm, Holiday Fenoglio Fowler, ranked slightly ahead. Stoffer bristles with the ranking. "They combine their debt and equity numbers; we don't," he says. "As a capital markets platform, if we combine equity and debt, we did well over $30 billion domestically in equity business, and that would make us super number one."

A VARIED BUSINESS

The 2004 numbers were very good, up nicely from the $11 billion in originations the previous year, and that includes almost every category of real estate: apartment, hotel/motel, industrial, mini-warehouse, mobile home, office, retail, and other special-purpose buildings. "The volumes we have today far exceed any dreams we had five years ago," says Stoffers.

The capital sources represented by L.J. Melody remain very diversified, including bank, credit company, FHA, Freddie Mac, Fannie Mae, life company, pension fund, private investor, real estate investment trust, savings and loan, and conduit sources. In 2004, the company worked with almost 200 different lenders.

"Before we merged with CB we used to do loans with five different lenders," says Melody, "and at the end of the year we would have done $1 billion. It used to be if you wanted to make a loan with Cigna, Texas Teachers (pension), New York State Teachers (pension), Metropolitan Life, or GE Capital, you would come to us. We were the eyes and ears of those lenders. Today, we are more exclusive with borrowers."

The company's average loan size is about $10 million, with transactions ranging from $1 million to $600 million. Says Stoffers, "We do an interesting mix in terms of loan sizes; 66% of our business was under $10 million and represented 22 percent of our dollar volume, but we also did $4.4 billion in deals that averaged $100 million."

Recent deals include:

- Arranged financing in the amount of $53 million for the acquisitions of Novo Nordisk North American Headquarters in Plainsboro, New Jersey.

- Arranged financing in the amount of $79 million for Village Pointe, a retail lifestyle center in Omaha, Nebraska. The fixed-rate loan included a 10-year term, with a built-in construction feature to allow for the future development of the final building.

- Arranged financing in the amount of $29 million for an office property at 1100 17th Street in Washington, D.C. A fixed-rate, five-year loan was secured for the Class A office building built in 1963 with total net rentable space of more than 142,000 square feet.

- Arranged permanent acquisition financing in the amount of $5.7 million for Old Bakery Place in Bristol, Virginia.

"There are definitely synergies in becoming a national lender, because from the borrower's perspective we represent so many different lenders in different markets," says Stoffers. "There are some lenders that tell us they work cheaper on our business because the information we show them from market to market doesn't vary. And what that does is drive lower spreads and better structures."

Says Melody, "Whereas 10 years ago, we would have one lender, maybe two lenders, involved in a competition with other mortgage bankers or direct lenders now we spend a lot of time and effort controlling the business, doing our due diligence, underwriting analysis, putting together a professional package, and offering it up to the marketplace—all of the people we think are good candidates to finance the deal. When something does get financed, it does so at the right price with the right lender at that point in time."

With a national lender there are definitely economies of scale, Stoffers adds. "That is especially so with servicing, which is a very important piece of our pie. It is the after-the-sale customer service that brings the borrower back over and over again."

Another reason servicing is considered so important is that it is in itself a revenue generator and evens out the peaks and valleys of the mortgage business, which rises and falls as the cycles change.

A TRUE MAVERICK'S APPROACH TO EQUITY FINANCING

1. Capital sources for equity financing are no longer difficult to find.
2. Equity financing prefers big projects, but some companies will do deals as low as $5 million.
3. Like mezzanine debt, equity financing fills in the missing piece in the capital stack.
4. Equity finance investors prefer a minimum yield and a share of cash flow or capital gains.
5. Use leverage to spread your own capital into different projects.
6. Use equity financing when developing apartments.
7. Percentage of returns are based on percentage of investment.
8. When deals do well, the developer's interests are "promoted"–the percentage of the return increases.
9. Standards have loosened, so equity financing takes up more of the equity gap.

CHAPTER 6

A Very Useful Subsidy

Two decades ago, when the federal government eliminated most of the tax write-offs involving real estate, it left something valuable in the empty place, the low-income-housing tax credit. For developers who have the patience and capital to work through the process, LIHTCs have been a road to riches.

A deal from March 2005: Bank of America provided $8.6 million in financing to support the acquisition and rehabilitation of 160 apartments on the far south side of Chicago. The Illinois Housing Development Authority (IHDA) issued tax-exempt municipal debt to finance the project and provided federal low-income-housing tax credits, syndicated by Related Capital Company.

Broken into its numerous parts, the financing of the apartment transactions looked like this: Bank of America Securities funded a new mortgage loan by underwriting $7 million in tax-exempt bonds issued by the IHDA. In addition, Bank of America provided a $1.6 million tax-exempt, tax-credit, equity bridge loan. Finally, on top of all that, Related Capital invested almost $4 million in equity through the purchase of low-income-housing tax credits generated by the project.[1]

Notice the number of entities involved: two Bank of America units, the IHDA, and Related Capital Company. And this was a relatively simple low-income-housing tax credit (best known by its acronym, LIHTC) deal.

While writing this chapter, I called an old college friend who was heavily involved in affordable housing developments using LIHTC. After first assuring me that any developer, anywhere, can get into the LIHTC game, he added the caution that most don't. The reason is that the application process can be daunting. "It is a very technical application and requires a lot of financial data. The average developer could not do it right away," says my old buddy, Mitchell Friedman. "They would have to bring in a financial consultant, and there are a lot of legal requirements. The developer would need to have an attorney with skills specifically in Section 42 of the Internal Revenue Code. . . ." He continued to ramble on for another few minutes.

I then remembered that Stephen Ross, who founded New

York–based Related Companies, was one of the first to figure out LIHTC credits, made millions in the affordable-housing business and, to boot, had a background in tax law. Maybe that would also explain the complexity of the Related Companies business model, but more on that later.

Enacted as part of the 1986 Tax Reform Act, the LIHTC is a key means by which the federal government funds construction of new rental housing and the acquisition and rehabilitation of existing rental housing for low-income households.[2] The government— surprisingly and wisely—recognized an incentive was necessary, because rental income and returns from low-income-housing investments are often not enough to cover operating costs. It has been a very successful program over the course of almost two decades, funding more than a million rental units for low-income households. For-profit developers and nonprofit agencies that work in the LIHTC world, and there are many, find it a very lucrative niche.

Late in 2004, I met an old college roommate from my University of Florida days while visiting the Sunshine State. He told me about another old friend who was building affordable housing throughout the state and living a local version of the Trump life, fast cars, a rental in South Beach and vacations in Costa Rica. I called him.

As Mitchell Friedman explained, he got involved with affordable housing after Hurricane Andrew in 1992, then five years later with three other partners formed Miami-based Pinnacle Housing Group. Over the next eight years, Pinnacle Housing developed 20 affordable housing projects around Florida, with about 3,000 units. The company counts five more projects in the pipeline.

How does a LIHTC project work? First, it's the states, not the federal government, that distribute the tax credits, says Friedman. Every state designates an agency to administer the federal tax credit program. In Florida, it's the Florida Housing Finance Corporation, and this is the agency that companies like Pinnacle have to negotiate with to gain tax credits. "The competition is fierce," says Friedman, although his company has done well in being allocated tax credits. (As per federal law, the allocation priority should go to projects that serve the lowest-income families and should be structured to remain affordable for a lengthy period of time.)

APPLICATION PROCESS HINTS

According to the National Association of Housing and Redevelopment Officials (NAHRO) in Washington, D.C., "The application process is very competitive in most states," and it makes these recommendations:

- Contact the agency responsible for tax credit allocation in your state to learn about the application process and the criteria by which the agency awards credits.

- Contact someone in an agency similar to yours who has gone through the application and allocation process, or find a consultant, especially if this is your first attempt.

- Know the rules. Some states accept applications continuously throughout the year, while others accept them only at specific times.

- Know the biases. Tax credit applications are awarded points for criteria outlined in the state's allocation plan. As an example, one state may give priority points to projects that offer units to tenants with special needs or that offer affordable units to tenants with very low incomes. In addition, states can enact (after holding public hearings) policies to target local problems such as distressed urban neighborhoods.

- Projects generally are awarded points and, as expected (but there are exceptions!), the developments that receive the highest number of points receive allocations.[3]

In a typical Pinnacle Housing development, about 50 percent of the capital comes from a first mortgage, usually through a local bank, and then 15 percent from local or state governments with programs to support the development or retention of low-income housing. The remaining 35 percent comes from the LIHTC. Here's how the latter piece works: A developer such as Pinnacle turns to a syndicator, like a Related Capital Company, that sells the tax credits. Fannie Mae is the largest buyer of tax credits in the country, but many big corporations (General Electric, oil companies, telecommunications firms, etc.) acquire them to reduce their own tax burden.

Specifically, those big corporations obtain a dollar-for-dollar reduction in their federal tax liability in exchange for providing equity to finance the development of qualified, affordable rental housing. That is, the corporations receive a tax write-off by using the tax credits, claimed in equal installments over a 10-year period, to offset taxes owed.[4]

If you look at the capital structure of the Pinnacle Housing LIHTC financing example, it's obvious why a developer likes these kinds of projects—the amount of debt needed is much, much lower level than for a free-market development.

That being said, the barriers to entry are relatively high, Friedman cautions. The two necessities are capital and time. In a free-market development, the builder will go the bank, borrow money, and then start work. With a LIHTC deal, it could take as long as 18 months to get the tax credits; in the meantime, you still have to do the preliminary work on the land, including site planning, environmental preparation, financial analysis, design, and, of course, dealing with the tax lawyers.

"A lot of people don't do it because they don't want the hassle of the application process," says Friedman. "But there is no secret to it. It just takes hard-nosed real estate development savvy. You have to have a good location and you have to know the application process."

TAX REFORM

Before the Tax Reform Act of 1986, billions of dollars were invested in real estate by investors mainly interested in tax-sheltered investments. Many investments were based on the concept of "accelerated depreciation," wherein real property could be depreciated over artificially short periods of time, with a large percentage of tax write-offs being taken in the early years. These substantial tax benefits were sold to investors through the sale of limited partnership shares. Investors gobbled them up, not because they made any economic sense but because of the tax write-offs.[5]

The Tax Reform Act did away with these tax shelters, but the government did give something back in the way of the LIHTC, which got under way in 1987; however, it wasn't made permanent by Congress until 1993.

The LIHTC is based on Section 42 of the Internal Revenue Code and provides a credit against tax liability as a dollar-for-dollar reduction in the amount of liability. Today, these tax credits have become the single most important source of capital subsidy in the development of affordable rental housing.[6] Each year, tax credits provide incentives for about $6 billion of private investment to help finance the production of approximately 120,000 apartments that have rents affordable to low-income families and individuals.[7]

The state allocations for tax credits continue to rise. Until 2000, each state received a tax credit of $1.25 per person that it could allocate toward funding housing that meets program guidelines. The per capita allocation jumped to $1.50 in 2001 and to $1.75 in 2002. In 2004, the number again rose, this time to $1.80, with the minimum of $2,075,000 going to the smallest state.[8]

HOW IT WORKS

Tax credits may be used for new construction, rehabilitation, or acquisition, and the projects must meet the following requirements:

- Either (1) 20 percent or more of the residential units in the project are both rent restricted and occupied by individuals whose income is 50 percent or less of area median gross income; or (2) 40 percent or more of the residential units in the project are both rent restricted and occupied by individuals whose income is 60 percent or less of area median gross income.[9]

- Rents charged by developers can be no more than a maximum of 30 percent of the income ceiling (i.e., maximum rents for LIHTC units are no more than 30 percent of either 50 percent or 60 percent of the area median income) mandated by the program.[10]

- Projects need to meet eligibility requirements for 30 years.

- Most new construction and substantial rehabilitation projects are eligible for a 9 percent tax credit (i.e., a credit equal to 9 percent of qualified costs each year for 10 years). For example, in a rehabilitation project with $100,000 in qualified costs, tax credits can equal $90,000 over 10 years. Projects that are financed through issuance of tax-exempt bonds may qualify for an automatic 4 percent tax credit allocation. Credits awarded to these projects are not subject to the per capita limit; however, the underlying bonds are subject to the state private activity bond cap.[11]

KEEP TO QUALITY

Friedman tells me that the affordable housing projects his company works on are not distinguishable in appearance from other free-market developments, with similar amenities (pool, clubhouse, library, exercise room, etc.).

This is the same point Stephen Ross, founder and chairman of The Related Companies, makes. "Affordable housing is no different than any other sector of real estate. You have to understand what is happening in the market. You have to do the project in a quality way. You want to do the best you can. Later, it will enhance your reputation and ability to get financing."

New York–based Related still does some tax credit deals in New York and Chicago, plus it owns 18 percent of publicly traded CharterMac (Ross holds the title of chairman), which is now the parent of Related Capital Company. CharterMac, also based in New York, invests in and services tax-exempt, multifamily mortgage bonds. As Hoovers.com notes, "Borrowers use the proceeds to finance multifamily housing, particularly properties meeting low income housing tax credit requirements."

THE SYNDICATORS

In 2002, Related Capital Company and affiliates provided $24 million of debt and equity financing to Atlanta-based Capital Development Group for a multifamily project in Savannah, Georgia, called The Oaks At Brandlewood. The way the deal worked out, Related Capital provided $9.9 million of equity investment for the tax credits generated by the development. CharterMac provided $13.9 million in financing through the purchase of bonds.[12]

As noted, after a project has been awarded tax credits, the owner or developer hires a syndicator such as Related Capital (as in the aforementioned deal), to market the credits.

Tax credit syndicators are a set of specialized investment banking firms that raise funds from corporate investors and reinvest those funds, often in pools, in a set of tax credit projects (such as The Oaks At Brandlewood). Tax credit syndicators compete with each other to secure investment capital from corporate investors and to purchase LIHTC in individual projects. A syndicator is not just the middle player in the deal; it also performs due diligence on behalf of the investor. In addition, it provides compliance-monitoring services for the investor or pool of investors for the duration of the compliance period. There is, of course, a cost. Syndicators charge investment banking fees that come out of the investment capital, lowering the net amount to be paid into the project's limited partnership."[13]

LIHTC, which must be taken over a 10-year period, are sold to investors on the basis of their current value. For example, a project may be awarded $1 million in tax credits, but, as the tax credits are spread out over a decade, investors typically discount the value to about $0.75 or $0.85 on the dollar. This means that $1 million in tax credits actually generates $750,000 to $850,000 in equity for the development (minus the syndication costs).[14]

Syndicators aren't the only game in town. Developers can also do a private placement, that is, a direct investment by a single corporate entity. In either case, when dealing with a private placement or syndicator, it's best to prepare a package of information on the project that includes some of the following: general partner background, operating budgets for the project, market study, site location map with photographs, and resumes for key members of the development team.[15]

DON'T STINT ON QUALITY

"Low income and affordable housing are the same," Ross explains. "It all started out as low-income and subsidized housing, but the government took away the subsidies. The only real subsidy left is the low-income tax credit, which today is called *affordable housing*. It is still something this country needs."

Although both The Related Companies and CharterMac (2004 revenues of $645.2 million) are no longer small organizations, Ross stresses, "Most of the industry is still with small developers. That is what the country needs. It is a great place to start and learn the business."

Affordable housing projects are generally in the range of 50 to 200 units, and, a with any other type of real estate, it's a matter of finding the best location. Often, the community will help, plus, as in the example Friedman laid out, the local government will contribute some "soft money."

"You want to build in a quality way, so when people look at it, they cannot discern that it is affordable housing," says Ross. "That was my philosophy, that people want to be proud of where they live. When we built our initial subsidized and lower-income projects, we put in sod, used good architecture, and we really provided a quality project."

He adds, "Real estate is a business and as with any business you have to look at every detail. Someone who understands details and enjoys building, that is what it takes to develop affordable housing."

SOARING HEIGHTS

Back in the 1970s, The Related Companies made its name in quality, multifamily, government-assisted housing developments, but over the subsequent three decades, Stephen Ross has made the world almost forget the company's origins. The Related Companies has become a complex, multifaceted real estate development, management, and finance company known for some of the most recent, high-profile developments in urban centers.

MEET THE MAVERICKS

Stephen M. Ross

Birth Date: 1940

Occupation: Founder, Chairman, and Chief Executive of The Related Companies; Chairman of CharterMac

Education: BA, accounting, University of Michigan; JD, Wayne State University; LLM, taxation, New York University.

Career Highlights:

- Founded Related Housing Companies
- Transformed Related Housing into The Related Companies
- Founded Related Capital Company, the largest owner of multifamily housing in the country
- Sold Related Capital to CharterMax; owns 18 percent of CharterMax
- Developed the Time Warner Center in New York

Today, when people hear about The Related Companies, their first thoughts aren't in regard to affordable housing—no, it is for a project about as far from that type of development as a company can get. Some well-known development firms create millions of square feet of high-profile buildings, but never come close to creating a project that becomes a landmark almost from the day it opens. The Related Companies did that very thing when it built the Time Warner Center at Columbus Circle in Manhattan.

Already considered New York's new Rockefeller Center, the $1.7 billion, mixed-use development designed by David Chiles of Skidmore, Owings & Merrill features a major upscale shopping mall, a five-star hotel, business offices, television studio, concert hall, residential apartments, and probably a half dozen other features that I'm forgetting.

In the *Wall Street Journal*, Ada Louise Huxtable wrote that the Time Warner Center was "exactly what a New York skyscraper should be—a soaring, shining, glamorous affirmation of the city's reach and power, and its best real architecture in a long time. Its two tall towers rise from symmetrical lower sections rotated in a bow to the [Columbus] Circle, where the huge building morphs into pedestrian shops and restaurants at ground level. But the wonder is the delicacy, the elegance, of these perfectly calibrated, glittering glass facades, the suave, sharp-edged precision that is amazingly subtle and refined for a structure of this enormous size."

On my last three visits to the Big Apple, I made a stop at the Time Warner Center. Earlier in 2005, however, I was there for a different reason: to visit Stephen Ross, who was wise enough to move his offices to his new building after it was completed.

I had never interviewed Ross before, and we began our talk somewhat tentatively, but after a while, he found his groove and time passed quickly—too quickly. I could have stayed for days talking to him without ever getting bored. The man clearly can tell a tale or two about the real estate world.

FINDING THE UNEXPLOITED NICHE

Although he graduated from high school in Florida, Ross was born and spent his early years in Detroit. For some reason perhaps only he can explain, Ross has remained loyal to his Midwest heritage. He went to college at the University of Michigan in Ann Arbor and then entered law school at Wayne State University in Detroit.

He graduated from the University of Michigan in 1962, and his most important revisit occurred 32 years later. In an extraordinary gesture of generosity, he provided a $100 million gift to the University of Michigan Business School, now named the Stephen M. Ross School of Business. Two things to note about the gift: It was the largest donation ever to a U.S. business school, and it was the largest gift to the University of Michigan in its 187-year history. That's a loyal graduate.

Ross began his professional life as a tax lawyer in Detroit. The job didn't thrill him. "I wasn't meant to be a lawyer. It was a little slow for me. I wanted more action," he says.

In Detroit, Ross was working in a real estate department, practicing tax law, and over time he realized that his clients were coming to him for advice on more than just tax planning and legal opinions. He could see the money they were making based on his opinions. "I was also bored with Detroit, so I moved to New York," he says now.

Ross changed professions, making the transition into investment banking, first with a company called Laird Inc. and then with Bear Stearns, from which he was eventually fired. It was then Ross realized he wasn't cut out to work for anyone else. In 1972, he drew up a business plan for an organization to be known as Related Housing Companies and made his first foray into multifamily real estate.

From the start, Ross had a unique vision. He could see that the good money in real estate was to be made in development, but to be a successful developer you had to have a ready source of capital. This led him to also establish a financial side, where, relying on his skills as a tax lawyer, he began setting up syndicated tax shelters for investors.

Ross's business revolved around affordable housing—in those days it was called *subsidized housing*—because this arena was about as risk-free as you could get in real estate at that time. "The Federal Housing Administration would give out 90 percent loan-to-value for multifamily, and if you knew how to structure a deal you could get pretty close to 100 percent," Ross explains.

It was an interesting business plan, because Ross could take the fees earned from syndicating the tax shelters and plow them back into the development side of the company. Actually, it was a little more complicated. "In looking at the affordable housing industry, I could see it was being done by a lot of different people, but nobody had combined the different pieces under one structure," he says. "My idea was to be a syndicator of tax shelters, mortgage financier, and developer."

That was the foundation of The Related Companies. By the end of the 1970s, Related raised more than $40 million in equity to support more than 50 developments with a value in excess of $250 million. It remains today the largest provider of equity and debt for affordable housing in the United States.

When the 1970s finally climaxed, the company had developed more than 5,000 apartment units. Today, the company can boast of having developed 75,000 units all over the country.

"Through our financial side of the business we brought in the syndications and stayed on as general partner in all of this affordable housing," Ross notes. "Today, we are one of the largest owners of affordable housing." (Related doesn't have full ownership, mostly a small position, but as general partners of the syndications, or pools of capital, the company is in a position of control).

OPPORTUNITY FOR CHANGE

In the early 1980s, Related Housing was invited to participate in a huge redevelopment project for Miami Beach's South Shore area, which is best known today as South Beach. It was a massive, mixed-use project, and Related would do the affordable housing piece. Ross, a quick study, saw how the master developer had put the whole deal together, and he was not impressed by the skill level of the developer; but he *was* impressed by the potential for mixed-use on a grand scale. "I said to myself, if this guy could do it, anyone can," Ross chuckles today. Well not quite, because soon afterward, Related Housing got involved in another large mixed-use project in New York called Riverwalk. After eight years and about a $12 million investment, Ross watched with dismay as the project got killed under Mayor David Dinkins's administration.

By that time, however, Related Housing had become The Related Companies and was busy with office towers for big corporations. Among its many successful projects were the headquarter buildings for International Paper, Nestlé Foods, Computer Associates, Mutual of New York, Fortune Brands, and Revlon.

The Related Companies didn't abandon residential, but it did push into market-rate multifamily. "We were one of the first to use variable-rate financing in New York City," Ross says with pride.

After the 1986 tax law change, Ross adroitly moved from tax syndications to LIHTC. Not everyone was so quick on their feet. The post-1986 tax change environment gradually morphed into a deep real estate recession that lasted through the early 1990s and brought down (or at least buckled the knees of) some of the biggest real estate players in the world at the time, two prime examples being Donald Trump and Paul Reichmann.

"From 1990 to 1994 it was really about staying alive," Ross says. "To quote Sam Zell, the objective was to 'stay alive to '95,' which we did. Not only did we have a great relationship with our banks, but our structure helped. We had other sources of income, such as affordable housing, which is still a great market for us, and the fees from Related Capital. We had to reduce our staff by about 10 percent, but we kept going."

Ross laughs. "I can smile about it now, but it was not fun at the time."

Referring to my first book, *Maverick Real Estate Investing: The Art of Buying and Selling Properties Like Trump, Zell, Simon, and the World's Greatest Landowners,* he says to me, "You know, many of the people you wrote about in your book barely got through it. When the country came out of that recession, Related was still a decent size. We looked around and we had less competition, and that allowed us to become one of the country's largest developers."

In the 1990s, Ross decided to reorganize the company into three divisions: development, management, and financial services. The development and management groups are easy to figure. Development acquires and develops luxury housing, government-assisted housing, retail, commercial, and mixed-use properties. It operates through a number of business units: Related New York, Related Florida, Related California, Time Warner Center, Related Urban Development, Related Lodging, Related Retail, Related Apartment Preservation, and LR Development.

The management division does what the name implies, provides management services for residential apartment units and commercial and retail space.

It's on the financial side that things are unusual, because The Related Companies doesn't directly do financial services anymore.

A subsidiary, Related Capital was taken public in 2004, when Ross executed a reverse merger of some tax-exempt bond funds that the company was advising. Then in November 2003, The Related Companies LP sold Related Capital to CharterMac (formerly known as Charter Municipal Mortgage Acceptance), coming out with an 18 percent ownership position in the new, publicly traded company (American Stock Exchange), also called CharterMac. Related Capital has become a subsidiary of CharterMac. With its 18 percent ownership of CharterMac's stock, The Related Companies controls CharterMac, which though independent is also, in effect, the financial services arm of The Related Companies.

CharterMac, under the capable hands of co–chief executive officers Stuart Boesky and Mark Schnitzer, has taken on all the complexity that was once The Related Companies. Under its umbrella, CharterMac offers financing for every part of the multifamily capital structure. The company originates and underwrites loans, plus holds more than $19 billion of assets under management.

CharterMac's core business is investing in tax-exempt bonds for its own portfolio, the proceeds of which are used to finance the construction or rehabilitation of affordable housing throughout the United States.

Related Capital, which was founded in the 1970s, remains one of the country's premier, multifamily-financing services firms, with a strong focus on affordable housing. It is the largest owner of multifamily properties in the country, with ownership interest in more than 278,000 units. Related Capital's investor clients include some of the nation's most prominent institutional investors, including global investment banks, insurance companies, pension plans, and Fortune 500 companies. In addition, the company offers an unparalleled asset management track record, critical to sectors such as LIHTC properties that must adhere to strict guidelines over an extended life in order to maintain eligibility.

Another subsidiary called PW Funding underwent a few alterations in 2005. The mortgage banker offers multifamily developers a full complement of conventional and tax-exempt mortgage products for market-rate and affordable multifamily properties. When CharterMac in 2005 purchased Capri Capital Finance, a commercial mortgage banking firm then ranked number seven in the country, for $84 million, it merged it into PW Funding, with the immediately bigger subsidiary changing its name to CharterMac Mortgage Capital Company.

Finally, CharterMac manages American Mortgage Acceptance Co., a publicly traded mortgage REIT that invests in government-insured mortgage loans.

Despite projects like the Time Warner Center, The Related Companies itself has not abandoned its roots. One of its direct business units, Related Apartment Preservation, intends to become the largest firm in the country in conserving affordable housing—that is, buying old projects, rehabbing them, and keeping them as affordable housing.

"We just bought [in 2004] Manhattan Plaza, one of the largest affordable housing communities in the country, 1,700 units of Section 8 housing, and preserved it," says Ross.

Manhattan Plaza featured two residential towers, with 70 percent of the units occupied by qualified performing artists. According to press reports, the purchase price was $155 million.

"Everybody was concerned about the project," Ross says. "I got hundreds of letters pressuring me to keep it as affordable housing. I could have sold those off as luxury condos based on the location, but the fact that we preserved it as affordable housing made a lot of people happy—and that was very important."

Second, The Related Companies is not a merchant builder. It considers itself an investor builder. It owns and manages all the projects it has built. Over time, that has become a reward. "When we did all that affordable housing using syndicated tax shelters, we stayed on as general partner," Ross says. "Now, 20 years later we are doing the refinancing on those same projects."

The Related Companies business has gone national. The company counts residential and retail developments in New York, mixed-use developments in West Palm Beach and Los Angeles, residential in Boston, and the furniture mart in Las Vegas; and due to its Chicago acquisitions, the company has become the top condominium developer in that city, in addition to running affordable housing there. The Related Group of Florida, says Ross, "is probably the largest condo developer in the country with over $8 billion under development."

Ross continues, "I'm going to do a lot of important projects, but the most important building I will ever do is the Time Warner Center because of its location in New York and the fact that it is such a large mixed-use project—I will probably never do another building that has so many uses. I think it will be an icon of New York in the twenty-first century and one of the most important building projects for which I will be recognized."

After Ross made that statement, I knew it was about time to wrap up my interview with him. As he saw me begin to close my notebook and get ready to turn off my recorders, he stopped me. "You didn't ask me what was the best thing I ever did." I was a little confused because I had assumed the best thing was the Time Warner Center. It wasn't.

"The best thing I ever did," he says, "was giving my gift of $100 million to the University of Michigan Business School. There is nothing better than having the opportunity to give back."

A TRUE MAVERICK'S APPROACH TO LOW-INCOME-HOUSING CREDITS

1. LIHTC deals usually involve numerous capital sources.
2. The application process is complex; use a consultant or lawyer with a specialty in this field.
3. The federal LIHTC program is administered by state agencies; know the state rules because each state does it slightly differently.
4. Local agencies can supply "soft money" to a deal.
5. The LIHTC process is lengthy; two requirements are capital and time.
6. Syndicators are used to actually deal the tax credits.
7. An alternative to syndicators is to do a private placement.
8. Investors usually get a small percentage discount when acquiring LIHTC.
9. LIHTC developments must meet rigid requirements.
10. The LIHTC program provides the single most important source of capital subsidy in the development of affordable rental housing
11. Although projects might be defined as affordable housing, developers should ensure that they have the same quality as free-market apartment complexes.
12. Corporate complexity is not always a bad idea.

CHAPTER 7

Turning Real Estate into Capital

Corporations long ago figured out how to monetize real estate assets, using the resulting capital for other purposes such as expansion. The concept is called a *sale-leaseback* and could easily be used by smaller businesses as well. Investors like these kinds of deals because they result in steady, long-term returns.

Earlier chapters have been about raising capital to invest in real estate. But suppose you had the capital in hand and were looking for something different—less risk on your investment. Unfortunately, less risk usually means lower return, so you'd want something else as the payoff—and that would be a consistent income stream.

Let's say you had a friend who had a successful business but was in need of capital for expansion purposes. You two meet for latte and scones one morning to discuss his plight. A thought occurs to you. He will sell you his corporate office, a beautiful, three-story building in Scottsdale, Arizona, and in return he will lease it back from you for a minimum of 15 years. The transaction solves two problems: You get your lower-risk real estate investment that comes with a steady income stream, and he gets the capital to expand his company.

That deal in a very basic way is called a *sale-leaseback* and has been used by corporations for decades as a way to monetize real estate on the balance sheet.

In 2001, I wrote an article that began with a perfect illustration of a sale-leaseback transaction. Galyan's Trading Company Inc., a sporting goods retailer, at that time operated 19 stores in the Midwest, and five of those stores were owned by a company that specialized in sale-leaseback transactions, W. P. Carey & Co. LLC., which had acquired the stores and then leased them back to Galyan's. What made this particular deal interesting was that Galyan's had built a 144,000-square-foot addition to its existing distribution facility in its hometown of Plainfield, Indiana, and that, too, was acquired by W. P. Carey.

I wrote at the time: "The expansion of the Plainfield distribution center exemplifies how companies such as W. P. Carey, using net lease deals, can expediently meet a growing company's particular need for financing. An original acquisition, which involved the purchase of five facilities operated by Galyan's, included an agreement with the retailer to fund the expansion of the distribution center. That transaction not only provided attractive financing, but enabled Galyan's to accommodate future growth."

ACQUISITION AND PROPERTY LEASE SYMBIOSIS

Okay, let's look at the sale-leaseback. Here are a few definitions in ascending order of complexity.

- In a typical sale-leaseback transaction, the funding source acquires a property and leases it back to the former owner on a triple net lease basis.

- The definition I use is similar. The property owner sells its real estate at fair market value to an investor, who then leases the property back to the previous owner under a long-term triple net lease. Unlike typical leased-space situations, where rents are based on fair market values, in a sale-leaseback the rent is based on the purchaser's financing costs and a market rate of return on the equity investment.

- Finally, here's the W. P. Carey version. The sale of a corporate headquarters, distribution facility, manufacturing facility, laboratory, or other physical property that will continue to be used by the seller. The divested asset can include a specific property in a single location or multiple properties in a number of locations. As part of the arrangement, the former owners lease the facility back from the purchaser for a period of time—typically 10 to 25 years—and the seller remains in control of the property.[1]

RENTAL RATE BALANCE

As I mentioned, sale-leaseback deals are usually done as a triple net lease. This means the seller-lessee remains responsible for all operating expenses, insurance, taxes, and maintenance of the property. By not including these costs in the base rent, the triple net lease gives the tenant more control over these variable costs.[2]

One benefit to the seller is that these deals are usually done for cash.

The two moving parts in the sale-leaseback transaction are, obviously, the sale price of the property and the rate at which the seller rents back the property.

In a typical deal, the property owner sells the real estate to an investor, who then leases the property back to the previous owner under a long-term lease, usually 15 to 20 years with multiple renewal options. This allows the seller-lessee to maintain complete control over the operation of the facility, the same as with ownership, for its useful life while benefiting from the use of the cash from the sale.[3] Unlike a typical space lease in which rents are based on fair market value, in a sale-leaseback, the rent is based on the purchaser's financing costs and a market rate of return on the equity investment.

There should be nothing unusual in the sale price. Have an independent appraiser evaluate the property to come up with a market value. However, the lease rate can be tricky. It represents the amount of rent the seller-tenant will pay and is largely dependent on the financial strength, or credit, of the tenant; the type of business the tenant is involved in; the location of the property; and the general condition of financial markets. Other factors affecting the lease rate include the buyer's cost of funds, the estimated residual value of the property at the end of the lease, and the tax benefits the lessor receives.[4]

LONG-TERM TENANT

From an investor's point of view, the truly great thing about sale-leaseback is that as long as the tenant is paying the rent, you will not get the property back for 10, 15, or 20 years, maybe longer. And the whole time, the property is throwing off a steady stream of income.

That is why you look at the credit of the tenant, says William Polk Carey, founder and chairman of W. P. Carey, because you want that tenant to be around 20 years after the moment you sign a deal. However, if something does go wrong, or if after 20 years the tenant decides to move elsewhere, you also want to make sure that property can be remarketed. Warns Carey, "You still have to look carefully at the real estate."

That's the balancing act: If the tenant is AAA-rated, then you don't need to focus on the real estate as much, but if the tenant carries significant credit risk, then the quality of the location is more important.

The key is to look at the credit of the tenant first and the real estate second, says Carey. "There are some exceptions where the real estate is deemed so beautiful that it can do nothing but go up in value. However, in a market like we have today where real estate is considered an answer to everyone's prayers, it's just a matter of time before real estate investments turn to curses."

Among W. P. Carey's long history of sale-leasebacks is a deal it did with a small high-tech company called Transcore Holdings Inc., a maker of radio frequency identification tags. It sold a 74,000-square-foot office and light industrial facility for $6.1 million and leased it back under a 15-year net lease—a home run for W. P. Carey. Conversely, a deal with another tech firm called Source Technology wasn't successful because it eventually went bankrupt. In the latter case, "The real estate rose to the occasion, and we did very well," says Carey. "Sometimes it does and sometimes it doesn't. You have to be prepared for both."

INCREASING POPULARITY

The volume of sale-leaseback deals passed $12 billion in 2003; that was up from $6 billion just two years before. A number of publicly traded real estate investments trusts—W. P. Carey, Commercial Net Lease Realty Inc., Lexington Corporate Properties Trust—specialize in the practice, and their deals involve all categories of business. These REITs are now fairly large in size. All three companies boast over a billion in assets.

Some REITs that don't specialize do them as well. In 2004, Five Star Quality Care Inc. sold 31 independent and assisted-living properties to Senior Housing Properties Trust for $148.2 million, then leased them back. Five Star made the move to raise funds for a $208 million acquisition of another company, LTA Holdings Inc.[5]

Some companies, such as Commercial Net Lease, hold to a very narrow focus. It usually looks for high-quality, freestanding retail properties with major tenants. It has done deals with Barnes & Noble, Eckerd, and OfficeMax.

Sale-leaseback deals have, in fact, been a staple of retailers, enabling them to better meet investor expectations, speed expansion plans, and be better poised to participate in merger and acquisition activity.[6] On the other side of the transaction, investors like sale-leaseback deals with major retailers because they want the stability of owning commercial properties occupied by national and regional tenants that are credit-rated. This part of the market is particularly appealing because there are few surprises. The investors know what the rent is going to be for 20 years.[7]

The trade-off with a sale-leaseback investment is that the returns are moderate, but the risk is less. A sale-leaseback investment offers investors a steady income stream with the added security of a hard asset behind the investment. Not all investments have to be shoot-for-the-moon. A stable return helps diversify any portfolio.[8]

A HOST OF BENEFITS

From an operating company perspective, the sale-leaseback has enjoyed a long history of financing expansion. It is in some regards an investment capital–generating technique. And, yes, while the larger national companies have traditionally used it effectively, it works equally well with established and growing small businesses.[9]

This is especially so with retail. For young companies, a sale-leaseback can quicken the pace of expansion. Traditionally, retailers grew on a store-by-store basis, and the growth pattern seemed inexorable. However, by using the largest-asset real estate on the balance sheet to gain capital, start-ups can expand at a quicker pace.

"More companies want to raise capital through a mechanism like a sale-leaseback. It's an alternative form of capital," noted Gordon DuGan, chief executive officer of W. P. Carey.[10]

Take the case of a Denver health club operator called Starmark Holdings. In 2003, it needed to raise capital, but didn't want to take on any more bank debt. It sold off 15 of its 33 Wellbridge health clubs for $178 million and leased them back under a 20-year agreement. At the time, one of the company executives remarked, "Rather than have capital tied up in real estate, we prefer to have capital to improve our club operations."[11]

Why would you want to do a sale-leaseback?

A couple of years ago, I wrote a story on sale-leasebacks and rattled off a number of benefits: (1) real estate doesn't create revenue for a company; (2) companies need capital to expand the core business; (3) manufacturers and service companies are not experts in real estate deal making and management and therefore should leave that part of the business to someone else; (4) ownership of real estate does not maximize assets; and (5) sale-leasebacks are increasingly seen as a viable alternative source of capital.

Let's look at some of these points starting with the last one, which is about dollars and sense. A sale-leaseback provides the release of capital, allowing a company to realize the full-market value of the real estate by increasing cash and off-balance-sheet action. It puts corporations on what is called the *efficient frontier* of capital. When added to the overall corporate financial mix, the sale-leaseback becomes part of the total capitalization.[12]

For point 4, I turn to a company called InterWest Commercial Mortgage in Austin, Minnesota, which does sale-leaseback financing starting at $3 million for a single-tenant deal. One of its selling points: There is a huge benefit on the sale in cases where the property has an appraised market value greater than its depreciated book value. Only the original purchase price of depreciated value is listed on the company's balance sheet. InterWest even supplies an example, "If the property is listed at $3 million and has a current value of $10 million, the sale-leaseback price would be $10 million, strengthening the company's balance sheet immediately with the conversion of a $3 million illiquid asset into $10 million cash."[13]

Point 3 is fairly obvious. If you're a software company, for example, and own your offices, there's a whole lot of extra worries on your mind, from maintenance to leasing (if you don't use all your space) to tax accounting. Through a sale-leaseback you still control your own space, but real estate becomes someone else's headache.

For point 2, I turn to Edward LaPuma, chief investment officer at W. P. Carey, who notes that sale-leasebacks enhance a company's borrowing capacity to fund R&D or acquisition activity, in essence redirecting capital back to the business's core activity, whether the company creates software or distributes roofing tile. A sale-leaseback also provides benefits in financial reporting, as the off-balance-sheet nature of the transaction allows a company to show an improved return on assets and an improved return on capital right away.[14]

As for point 1, unless you are in the business of real estate, you shouldn't be in the real estate business. Not only doesn't your property create revenue, but property is a liability, which is why fast-growing companies, such as technology firms, work diligently to get real estate off the books. When taking the next step, raising venture capital funds or even going public, a balance sheet without the real estate debt is cleaner and more attractive to capital sources. In short, if your company carries a mortgage instead of a lease, the mortgage would be listed on the balance sheet as a long-term debt, possibly having an adverse effect on future borrowing.

There are a number of surprising benefits to a sale-leaseback, at least compared to a conventional mortgage: (1) The sale-leaseback should provide the company with cash equal to 100 percent of the fair market value of the property, while conventional mortgage financing generally yields cash proceeds equal to 75 percent or less of the property's value; (2) when long-term interest rates are low, a sale-leaseback may enable the company to lock in a low cost of funds for a longer term than is available to the company through conventional financing; and (3) a company's ability to obtain a mortgage loan may be limited by state or federal regulations, or financial covenants under its existing credit facilities; in such cases a sale-leaseback may be the company's only mean of raising capital.[15]

VARIATIONS ON A THEME

It should be noted that a number of offshoots from the sale-leaseback concept have had periods of popularity. Regulation changes have made some of them less viable, but real estate lawyers are an ingenious bunch, and these kinds of complex variations always have a way of coming back.

The first offshoot is called the *credit tenant lease* (CTL) financing, which is based on the lease as opposed to the real estate.

Years ago, a Cohen Financial executive taught me the ins and outs of the CTL. He instructed me that you look to the strength of the tenant and then finance the real estate based on a combination of the real estate value and strong tenant. Or you can totally ignore the real estate. This type of deal can be very appealing to real estate developers because the financing is based on the terms of the lease. If there is a 20-year lease, for example, the developer is going to get a 20-year loan.

If all this sounds a little muddy, think of it this way. You have a project in which you lease space to one AAA-rated tenant. You then borrow dollars based on that lease deal. In the loan payback, the borrower redistributes almost all the rent that comes in under that lease toward debt service.

SECOND VARIATION

The 1990s saw the blossoming of a very unique financing mechanism called the *synthetic lease.* Again, it was popular with fast-growing technology and biotech industries and even some retailers because of its ability to take corporate real estate off the books even as a company kept control of the real estate and retained the tax benefits of ownership.

This financing technique gave sale-leasebacks heady competition in the hearts and minds of corporate financiers—only to crash and burn, not of its own doing, but because of one of the great corporate scandals of recent years: Enron!

I don't know if Enron did any synthetic leases, but the Enron mess was all about off-balance-sheet units called *special purpose entities* (SPEs), which were a key part of synthetic leases.

Here's the way it worked. The synthetic lease created an off-balance-sheet SPE to own the property in question. The financing entity, usually a bank, would often end up holding a small piece of

SPE ownership. The synthetic lease itself was short term, usually five to seven years, at the end of which was a balloon payment.

Specifically, in a synthetic lease arrangement, a corporation finds a lender who uses an independent leasing entity to finance new construction or the purchase of an existing single-tenant building. The leasing entity holds the title and leases it back to the corporation through short-term financing, requiring interest-only periodic payments and a balloon purchase payment due at the end of the term. During the lease term, the company deducts interest payments and property depreciation as expenses for taxes. However, for accounting purposes, the interest payments are considered rent as per a standard operating lease, keeping the property and debt off the balance sheet.[16]

The key advantages were numerous: It was really an inexpensive loan, because the interest rates were mostly tied to the London Interbank Offered Rate (LIBOR); the company maintained control of the property; there were no tax consequences; the balance sheet was clean (real estate was in the hands of the SPE); and it was relatively easy to do a deal.

There were numerous risks tied to the synthetic lease, however, and the biggest one had nothing to do with the structure itself. When Enron blew up, SPEs of all types became suspect, and groups such as the Financial Accounting Standards Board revisited those vehicles. In January 2003, FASB issued a pronouncement affecting off-balance-sheet assets, liabilities, and obligations. The net effect was that the synthetic lease became less useful in regard to real estate.

When the synthetic lease market petered out due to new accounting standards, the result was renewed demand for dedicated sale-leaseback finance companies, which had viewed synthetic leases as a competitive product.

Not that sale-leaseback companies needed any invigoration. They were already running hot. Over a five-year period, for example, W. P. Carey's assets under ownership and management jumped from $2.625 billion in 2000 to $7 billion at the end of 2004.

MEET THE MAVERICKS

William Polk Carey

Birth Date: 1930

Occupation: Founder and Chairman of W. P. Carey & Co. LLC

Education: BS, economics, University of Pennsylvania's Wharton School

Career Highlights:

- Founded Carey International, which brought the first foreign direct investment capital into Australia in 1960
- Founded W. P. Carey & Co.
- Took W. P. Carey & Co. public twice, which eventually became W. P. Carey & Co. LLC
- Used a sale-leaseback to help finance the buyout of Gibson Greeting Cards
- Endowed the W. P. Carey School of Business at Arizona State University

A PIONEER IN THE FIELD

W. P. Carey & Co. was founded in 1973 by William Polk Carey after a long career of entrepreneurship and investment banking.

Carey's parents owned a summer place in France during the Depression years, and since it was cheaper at the time to live in France than in the United States, they resided there; but in 1930, the family made a quick trip back to the United States so their child, William Polk, could be born in the United States.

After his parents divorced, his mother relocated to Baltimore and eventually married a Texas oilman. Despite what seemed like a moneyed-class existence, Carey worked to put himself through college, running a secondhand refrigerator business while attending Princeton. Eventually he had to leave Princeton because he was spending too much time on the business and not enough in class.

By that time, his mother had married for a fourth time, to a man who was one of the first automobile dealers for Chrysler. His new stepfather struck a deal with Carey. He would pay for college—which turned out to be the University of Pennsylvania's Wharton School—if Carey would come to work for him for three years after graduation. After a two-year stint in the U.S. Air Force during the post–Korean War years, that's what happened. (Carey ended up affiliated with several Ivy League schools. In addition to his academic forays into Princeton and the University of Pennsylvania, in 1999 he served as the executive in residence at Harvard Business School.)

Carey and his stepfather formed a company called International Leasing Corporation. From lessons he learned in that business, Carey in 1959 started a small, international investment banking firm called Carey International, mostly doing debt placement and other types of financing. Among his accomplishments with Carey International was bringing the first foreign direct investment capital into Australia in 1960.

The company was successful enough that a bigger firm, Hubbard, Westervelt & Mottelay (now Merrill Lynch Hubbard), acquired Carey International, giving Carey 15 percent of the merged company. Beginning in 1964, Carey served as chairman of the merged company's executive committee and moved it into the net leasing of corporate real estate.

Carey then changed jobs, moving to Loeb, Rhoades & Co. (now part of Lehman Brothers), where he served as head of real estate and equipment financing, then to duPont Glore Forgan Inc. as chairman and director of corporate finance.

After more than a decade in the investment banking industry, Carey decided in 1973 to strike out on his own one more time, forming W. P. Carey & Co., primarily to structure single-asset, private investments. Its specialty was lease financing. "There were only a few other players in the field, because few people knew of it," says Carey. "We did private placement of debt and sale-leasebacks. It was a good business from the start."

It was so good that Carey almost ran out from under his own equity. "After two or three years, I was running out of money," he says. "I had deals in the pipeline, but no cash."

At first he considered merging his company with First Boston, but the terms were onerous. That's when family stepped in. Carey's brother-in-law, who had at one time been married to J.P. Morgan's granddaughter, pulled him aside and said, "Don't merge with First Boston. If you run out of money, I'll come to your aid." Says Carey, "It was great. We got some deals closed and everything from then on moved along fine."

Looking back, Carey notes, "It always takes longer than you think to turn a profit. Yet it was steady growth for us. Eventually, E.F. Hutton expressed interest in distributing some of our product and did so for several years."

A BUYOUT OPTION

The deal that put W. P. Carey on the map was the buyout of Cincinnati-based Gibson Greeting Cards in 1982. William Simon, former Treasury secretary in the Nixon administration, had formed an investment banking firm called Wesray Corporation. His company bought Gibson Greeting for around $81 million, of which Wesray ponied up a mere $1 million. Sixteen months later, Wesray sold 17 percent of Gibson Greeting to the public for $45 million—all cash.

Where did Simon get the other $80 million to make the deal? Partly from W. P. Carey & Co. Wesray sold Gibson Greeting's 3 million square feet of buildings to W. P. Carey for $35.4 million and then leased back the space.

Carey gives credit for the transaction (which was a big deal at the time) to his chief investment officer, George Stoddard. "It looked too highly leveraged and I didn't want to touch it," he says. "But George was able to see the beauty of it; in particular, he could see that Simon was buying at a very reasonable price, so the value of the company was more than he was paying for it. Our coverage was more than adequate."

Wesray wasn't the only investor to use the sale-leaseback to finance a buyout. Also in the last decade, W. P. Carey acquired four buildings from the Detroit Diesel Corporation for $41 million. The proceeds were used to finance the buyout of Detroit Diesel by Roger Penske from General Motors.

"Some deals turned out to be home runs, like Gibson Greeting, but others did not," says Carey. "Still, in balance, things turned out really well."

The buyouts were unique because the real estate was treated as a separate, valuable entity. "It was an interesting approach," Carey explains, "to simply say the companies don't seem to be worth very much, but the real estate is."

He adds, "It takes a great deal of analysis to see what the real estate is worth. We looked hard at the properties and could see they were valuable, but whenever you have a property that is leased to a single company you have a lot of risk, because if that company goes out of business, it may or may not take the properties. You may get back a piece of real estate tied to a single purpose. You have to be careful in analyzing the long-term prospects."

The good thing about Simon was that he was as careful in considering its takeover targets as Carey was in regard to real estate. W. P. Carey & Co. ended up doing seven deals with Wesray.

ROLLING UP LIMITED PARTNERSHIPS

Back in 1979, Carey decided to attack the issue of raising capital by launching a series of limited partnerships under the Corporate Property Associates banner. These funds were built around single-tenant properties acquired through sale-leaseback transactions.

With the tax law changes in 1986, a lot of limited partnerships began to go belly-up, mostly because they had been constructed for tax-loss purposes. "Almost all the real estate limited partnerships went bad," Carey recalls. "Ours didn't, because they were built to make money for the investors, not to experience losses for tax purposes. There was nothing intrinsically wrong with limited partnerships, but for many years they were looked down on because so many went bad."

By 1997, there were nine Corporate Property Associate funds, and they had invested in 197 properties with an approximate value of $750 million. The next year, Carey consolidated them all into Carey Diversified LLC and went public, trading on the New York Stock Exchange. Two years later, in June 2000, Carey Diversified acquired its manager, W. P. Carey & Co., and created W. P. Carey & Co. LLC.

The Corporate Property Associates series continues to this day, with the most recent fund carrying the number 16. All told, W. P. Carey owns and manages more than 700 commercial and industrial properties comprising 90 million square feet. The value of all those buildings totals about $7 billion.

In 2004, the company reported total revenue of $227.8 million, up from $159.2 million for the same period in 2003; net income rose to $63.9 million, a slight increase from $62.9 million for the same period in 2003—which only goes to prove that a sale-leaseback is not an automatic money machine.

Corporate Property Associates wasn't inactive in 2004; on behalf of the series, W. P. Carey completed $890 million in investments, up nicely from $725 million in 2003. W. P. Carey also managed an affiliated REIT called Carey Institutional Properties, but in 2004 it was liquidated, with the company acquiring 17 office, industrial, retail, and warehouse properties from CIP for approximately $142 million, which included the assumption of $28 million in debt.

I finally got to meet Carey in person at the end of 2004 when he was hosting an affair at Arizona State University. Actually, ASU's school of business was holding the affair with Carey as the host, because in January 2003, the W. P. Carey Foundation endowed the school with $50 million. Today, various business degrees are now offered at the Arizona State University W. P. Carey School of Business.

The endowment of a business college in Arizona ties together a number of ancestral threads for Carey. His family tree includes Joseph Wharton, founder of the Wharton School at the University of Pennsylvania, and Leonidas Polk, who helped found the University of the South in Sewanee, Tennessee. Carey's grandfather was on the first board of Johns Hopkins Hospital, and another relative was the first chairman of the hospital. Johns was his mother's maiden name. The Arizona connection? His grandfather was a legislator during the 1880s for the Arizona Territory.

PASSING THE BATON

In 2005, the year in which Carey turned 75, it was my time to finally interview him in person for this book. The W. P. Carey

offices overlook Rockefeller Center in Manhattan, and for our dis-
cussion about sale-leasebacks Carey invited me to lunch at one of
the corporate offices. The formal and elegant lunch was served by a
single waiter who silently placed each course before us and disappeared as spontaneously as she appeared.

On the eve of his seventy-fifth birthday, Carey relinquished his
role as chief executive officer of the company he founded. Gordon
DuGan, at age 38, roughly half the age of Carey, succeeded him.
Carey's gentlemanly expression of good wishes was, "With the
approach of my seventy-fifth birthday, this was a natural time to further our transition plans, providing the youthful, vigorous leadership of Gordon DuGan."[17]

Carey, of the old school, was dressed for our lunch in formal business attire, with a crisply knotted tie complementing what looked
like a Fallan and Harvey suit. Unlike boisterous real estate investors
like Donald Trump who try to dominate a room, Carey talks in a
very low, modulated voice, almost a whisper. Then again, he never
considered himself a real estate man. As he told me more than once,
he was always a financial guy.

As a "financial guy," Carey built his company through a carefully
thought-out, conservative game plan. While the sale-leaseback is, on
the surface, a very simple financial maneuver, not everyone does it
well. Carey notes, "There were some studies as to how net lease deals
performed, and what they found out was they were not all the same.
There was no pattern."

Actually, there was one pattern: W. P. Carey outperformed every
other company doing sale-leasebacks.

Carey tells this story. Years ago, someone from his company visited a potential client in Japan. At the time, W. P. Carey was the
second- or third-largest firm doing sale-leaseback deals, and that
wasn't good enough for the Japanese firm. It considered itself the
biggest at what it did and only wanted to deal with the biggest

sale-leaseback company, Integrated Resources. Unfortunately for the Japanese, Integrated Resources soon went out of business.

"We had a visit from one of the agencies, I think it was Moody's," Carey remembers. "At the time they were still giving Integrated Resources an investment grade. As it turned out, it was a few days before Integrated Resources declared bankruptcy."

The sale-leaseback business has gotten very busy since the turn of the millennium, which is one reason why W. P. Carey has been looking to do deals overseas in recent years. The company has been active in Europe, doing sale-leaseback transactions in Finland, the Netherlands, Germany, France, and Belgium. Other countries where it has properties include England, Canada, Ireland, Sweden, and Thailand.

After a recent deal in Europe, LaPuma, the company's chief investment officer, noted the transaction represented W. P. Carey's commitment to provide sale-leaseback financing to international companies. "As we continue to expand our presence in the European market, we will seek quality investments with companies across the credit spectrum in order to further diversify our investors' investment portfolios while providing our tenant-clients the ability to monetize their real estate assets. We anticipate an increase in our investment volume in the months ahead as more European companies realize the benefits of customized financing solutions."[18]

Having been in the sale-leaseback business for three decades, Carey suddenly finds what was once a lonely, quiet business transformed into the usual hustle of generic real estate promotion.

This business, Carey stresses, is a long-term business. "Too many people are going into net leasing, and they probably are going to be out of it in the next few years."

A TRUE MAVERICK'S APPROACH TO SALE-LEASEBACKS

1. Sale-leasebacks monetize real estate so that capital can be used elsewhere.
2. These deals allow you to acquire property and then lease back to the seller.
3. All deals are done on a triple net lease basis.
4. Leases are long term.
5. These arrangements produce steady income stream for a 20-year period.
6. The rent structure is based on financing costs, rate of return, and credit strength of tenant.
7. These deals release capital.
8. The tenants retain control of the property.
9. Sale-leasebacks are useful for companies who want to get out from under the burden of property management.
10. With real estate off the books, a company's balance sheet looks a lot cleaner.
11. These arrangements compare favorably to conventional mortgages.
12. They can be used to raise capital in a corporate buyout.
13. There is lots of competition to do sale-leaseback deals.

CHAPTER 8

Retail Site Arbitrage

When a major retailer begins to stumble, panic grips those companies that have outstanding credit issues with the chain of stores. A number of astute real estate investors have a different interpretation of these events and often come to the financial aid of the retailer. Investors don't do this for altruistic reasons, but to hedge their own landlord/tenant relationship or to gain outright control of store locations.

In the course of writing this particular chapter of the book, I've been following the winding down of the kids' emporium, Toys "R" Us. Although it seems as though the store has been with us forever—at least for me because I often wandered the Toys "R" Us aisles when my children were growing up—it became a public company only in 1978, so as an American shopping icon, it lasted less than three decades.

As a specialty retailer, Toys "R" Us became the largest toy seller in the United States. Then, with the growth of Wal-Mart, shopping patterns changed. Not only did Wal-Mart supplant Toys "R" Us as the largest toy seller, its discount pricing slew a host of other toy retailers as well. When I pull out a *Wall Street Journal* of December 3, 2003, one of the headlines of the Marketplace section reads, "Storied FAO Is Casualty of Tough Holiday Toy-Pricing War." The story of FAO, Toys "R" Us, and other toy sellers can be summed up in this paragraph: "Discount retailer Wal-Mart Stores Inc. kicked off the holiday toy wars earlier than usual this year to generate traffic by offering steep discounts on popular items. Rivals, including Toys "R" Us, KB Toys and FAO, have found it increasingly difficult to match Wal-Mart's prices."[1]

There it is: three toy retailers killed by Wal-Mart. Of those three, only Toys "R" Us had freestanding stores; KB Toys and FAO were mostly mall stores. It is for that reason, as Toys "R" Us began its death spiral, a bidding war started up for the company. As I'm writing this chapter, the most recent news from the Toys "R" Us denouement is that shareholders have approved a buyout proposal to take the company private. The company is being taken over by a consortium of three investor groups, two private equity firms, and Vornado Realty Trust. It is assumed Vornado's interest was in the real estate.

Most of the financing topics discussed in this book work for any asset class. There are two exceptions: agency loans and low-income housing credits, which can be used only for multifamily or similar types of real estate such as housing for seniors. This chapter is also an exception in that the acquisition technique discussed here is solely about retail properties. It is technically not a financing structure, but more of a strategy.

There is not yet a formal or even colloquial name for the strategy, although it has been around for decades, so let's just call it *retail site arbitrage,* since it involves current lease rates versus future lease rates for an empty or soon-to-be-empty store currently in the folds of a failing retailer. The key to this strategy means establishing a financial relationship with an individual retailer to control the destiny of its real estate.

Toys "R" Us was in good company at midyear 2005, because investors had been chasing other retailers as well. Neiman Marcus and Saks were in play, and a private equity firm paid $715 million to buy discount-store-operator ShopKo Stores. All the financial players involved or potentially involved in these deals believed they could improve the fortunes of these retailers while at the same time take advantage of a thriving real estate market to sell a number of well-located stores.[2]

This interest in retail real estate reached a fever pitch early in the new century because of the success of one man, Edward Lampert, the head of a Connecticut hedge fund, who took control of the failed Kmart Corp. by acquiring the company's bonds during bankruptcy proceedings. Soon afterward, he sold 68 stores to Home Depot Inc. and Sears for $846.9 million, a total that was nearly as much as the $879 million value placed on all of Kmart's real estate—1,513 stores and 16 distribution centers—by the bankruptcy court.[3]

With Kmart again on solid footing and its stock climbing to over a $100 share, Lampert then acquired Sears department stores and merged the two to create a new Sears Holding Corp. Suddenly,

Lampert was a financial god, and his astute reading of the land value in regard to bankrupt retailers has since become an established game plan.

While Lampert deserves all the plaudits and notoriety for the Kmart and Sears deal, he wasn't by any regard the first to venture into this kind of strategy. There have been a number of pioneers in this field, including Steven Roth, chief executive of Vornado Realty Trust, who in 1995 bought a controlling interest in another failed retailer, Alexander's Inc., simply for the real estate it owned.

However, the true maverick in regard to retail land arbitrage is a twinkly, grandfatherly gentleman, who at 76 is still in charge of the company he founded more than 40 years ago. Milton Cooper holds tightly to the titles of chairman and chief executive officer of Kimco Realty Corp., a New Hyde Park, New York, real estate investment trust that invests in retail shopping space.

Back in the 1960s, Kimco formed a joint venture with a retailer called Zayre to own shopping centers in which Zayre would be one of the anchors.

Zayre was formed in 1956 as a discount retailer in the Northeast, but eventually expanded nationally. The company actually started the TJ Maxx and BJ's Wholesale Club chains, but later sold them off. Zayre became an early troubled retailer, with low-quality goods and outdated stores. In October 1988, the Zayre stores were sold to another retailer, Ames Department stores.[4] Cooper was a little fuzzy on the details, but says, "When Zayre went out of business, we bought them out of the partnership."

In any case, it was a maverick effort in retail site arbitrage, and an interesting strategy. In order to help Zayre expand, Kimco would develop shopping centers with Zayre as an anchor, and Zayre itself would be one of the investors in the shopping center developments. This was a good strategy at the time, but in today's world, retailers try not to own too much real estate, as it is a nonperforming asset on the balance sheet. In addition, a retailer wants to be a pure operating company as opposed to being a retailer plus a real estate investor and manager.

"I don't remember how many stores it [Zayre joint venture] involved, but it was a good deal for both of us," Cooper says. It must have been, because Kimco would pitch headlong into retail site arbitrage as a primary growth engine through 1990s when no one else but Vornado's Roth was even considering such a strategy. No company has been as aggressive as Kimco in going after these deals. The company even teamed up with Goldman Sachs Group Inc. to go after Toys "R" Us, but lost out to the temporary triumvirate of Vornado, Kohlberg Kravis Roberts & Co., and Bain Capital LLC.

The proposition in retail site arbitrage is that the real estate is, pardon the pun, an "underlying" value that the store itself is not capturing. So, how does an investor capture that hidden value? The obvious answer is to re-lease. Since most retailers lock into long-term leases, over time the face value of the lease appears "cheap," especially in a period during which real estate prices climb steadily. If, as an investor, you buy a portfolio of properties at a cost based on the value of the current leases, or if you are an excellent negotiator and buy at a discount, and if the tenant fails and you control the space, you would then be re-leasing the same space at a current lease rate that one assumes is much higher than when the retailer first signed a lease, thus immediately increasing the value of your investment. Again, this is all about maximizing the value and return of the underlying real estate.[5]

For retail site arbitrage to work, the location of the space has to be desirable for another tenant. Of the 900 locations in the Toys "R" Us deal, some are in very questionable strip-mall locations.[6]

As with any real estate investment, although the concept looks rewarding, a little research may prove otherwise, especially in the case of retail. Real estate on which shops are built has been one of the best-performing sectors since the turn of the millennium, and that was even before Lampert's Kmart coup. Since then, retail real estate has been hotter than a mall parking lot in July in Phoenix. The follow-up question remains, is there more upside to retail?

If the answer is no, one might have to deal with some very ugly competitive factors. During the endgame for Toys "R" Us, *Wall Street Journal* scribe Ray Smith wrote that while some investors such as Edward Lampert have been "able to unlock value in prime real estate that some retailers own, record numbers of stores are set to come on the market at the same time in the months ahead, which weighs on real estate prices."

Here are some issues to keep in mind in regard to retail site arbitrage:

- It unfolds through unlimited variations. The nature of the deal depends on the individual retailer and the real estate.

- Opportunities arise when retailers face an uncertain future.

- The buildings and/or land in question can easily be leased or sold to another user.

- Instead of bringing in capital through a loan, investors must use their own considerable resources to invigorate the retailer, even if it is just temporary.

- Since this is about control of a site, the acquisition can be either the property or just the leasehold.

- Failing retailers often present a smart investor with a series of opportunities.

- The strategy can be used in small, one-off investments, although it has mostly been employed by major players involving millions in outlay.

STRATEGIES

There are a number of ways to play in retail site arbitrage. A company like Kimco has tried most of them. Its aggressive strategy has been to hedge existing investments by making further investments in the retailer. Others use retail site arbitrage in different ways. For Lampert's investment in Kmart, the land was a fallback means to recoup initial capital outlay in case his plan to resurrect the retailer failed. With Kimco and Lampert, investments in the struggling retailer needed to be hedged to protect against the ultimate downside, the complete shuttering of stores. On the other hand, Vornado made an investment in a second company to control the real estate, which was all that was left after the retailer failed.

Strategy 1: The True Hedge

When Zayre folded, it sold its stores for $788 million to Ames Department Stores Inc., which at the time was a little-known New England retailer. The deal turned Ames into one of the nation's largest discount chains, but size didn't equate with success. Ames suffered from too much debt and couldn't get out from under its real estate because the property markets had begun to collapse—the beginning of a national real estate recession. Eventually, Ames would close about 74 stores and file for Chapter 11 bankruptcy.

Ames later emerged from bankruptcy protection and in 1998 bought a competitor, Hills Stores Co. The results of the expansion weren't any better than those experienced with Zayre. By 2001, Ames, heavily in debt from its purchase of the Hills chain and facing a deteriorating retail market, was scrambling to refinance and find new sources of capital.

As Ames drifted into bankruptcy once again, it was able to rework a $650 senior credit facility with GE Capital, and in what was even then termed "unconventional," the company arranged a $75 million credit line with Kimco that was secured by the leasehold interests on selected Ames stores. Kimco was the landlord at the time for 29 Ames stores. Dow Jones reported in 2002, "When it filed for bankruptcy protection last August, Ames was granted $755 million in DIP [debtor-in-possession] financing from the GE Capital Corp. division of General Electric Co. and Kimco Funding LLC, an affiliate of Kimco Realty Corp. But it had depleted those funds."[7]

Says Cooper, "Ames had valuable leases, but they were out of money. Since the lease had value, we made a loan secured by the leases with court approval. We got a percentage above what it felt the conservative value of the leases were. When Ames liquidated and sold the stores, it got cash, and the creditors received a better, enhanced distribution. It was a good deal for Ames' creditors."

Kimco entered into the financing of Ames to hedge its exposure to 29 Ames locations. The company did take a hit in occupancy when Ames went out of business, but the slap was temporary. In 2002, Kimco could report 9 stores where Ames still paid rent, 10 stores leased to grocery and discount store tenants, and 10 stores still seeking tenants.[8]

Strategy 2: The Importance of Real Estate

When Lambert first took over Kmart, he appeared to be making a pure real estate play, but after he sold off almost $850 million worth of store sites, he settled down to run a company.

What the sale did, however, was to put retail real estate on the map—but in a totally different context than it had been, except for a few mavericks like Kimco's Cooper and Vornado's Roth. Before Kmart, many property owners considered empty big-box stores to be scary, potential liabilities. After the Kmart deal, they were perceived as valuable assets. What made the Kmart properties particularly interesting was that they were mostly stand-alone sites or part of outdoor shopping centers. Therefore, those in good locations could be marketed to such fast-growing chains as Kohl's, Target, or even warehouse stores.

Business Week made the case that Lampert is actually a student of famed investor Warren Buffett, and to some extent it is right. Buffett used his investment in a fading textile maker called Berkshire Hathawy Inc. to launch his investment powerhouse. In a similar vein, Lampert went after Kmart. In 2002, with Kmart in Chapter 11 bankruptcy proceedings, Lampert's hedge fund, Greenwich, Connecticut–based ESL Investments Inc., started buying the company's debt. Creditors were all too willing to get out by selling to Lampert. At first it looked like the creditors were making the right move, as the retailer continued to slump, but Lampert stuck to his game plan, buying even more debt. Eventually, he accumulated enough stock to give him control of the bankruptcy process. After emerging as the largest shareholder, he became chairman. In the reorganization, all the debt was converted to cash. It's been reported that he took control of the $23 billion retail chain with less than $1 billion in investment.[9]

Unlike Buffett, who is simply an investor, Lampert took operational control of Kmart and then, with the Sears merger, became chief executive of Sears Holdings Corp.

Lampert had confidence in his moves because he had a fallback position. Remember, Kmart in 2002 boasted more than 1,500 stores. Just 68 of those were sold for the $846.9 million, which was close to what Lampert spent to take control of the company. As *Business Week* noted before the Sears deal, "Even if Kmart eventually fails, keeping it going as long as possible lets him extract top dollar for its valuable real estate by selling the stores over time."[10]

Strategy 3: Long-Term Control

Vornado Realty Trust's chairman and chief executive officer, Steven Roth, is known for his forward, gruff manner, but when it comes to business he can sit back and wait for the right opportunity to arise. When Alexander's, a Northeast-based department store chain, went out of the business, the surviving company held onto its real estate. After emerging from bankruptcy, it then morphed into Alexander's Inc., a Paramus, New Jersey–based REIT. In 1995, Vornado bought a controlling interest in the company, which really amounted to nothing more than six properties in New York and New Jersey totaling 1.3 million square feet.[11]

Vornado, a REIT that builds and owns office buildings and retail centers in the New York metro area, coveted one thing from Alexander's: the site of the former flagship store in Manhattan, which amounted to an entire city block. After lengthy negotiations with potential tenants and numerous changes in design, Vornado finally began building, six years after the investment, the 56-story high-rise officially known as 731 Lexington Avenue—but sometimes called the Bloomberg Tower because the financial information company rents 700,000 square feet and is the signature tenant for the building.

Vornado redeveloped and leased the remaining Alexander's sites. As a bonus to all that activity, the stock price of the once-defunct department store chain now trades above $250 a share.

A COMMON STRATEGY

The most common strategy in dealing with a troubled retailer, and one employed often by Kimco in the 1990s, has been to spot early on that a retailer, which might or might not be a tenant, has begun to suffer financial convulsions.

While creditors fear this type of situation, although it sounds macabre, retail land specialists should take notice and, if possible, move quickly to help, because that retailer could use a financial

MEET THE MAVERICKS

Milton Cooper

Birth Date: 1929

Occupation: Chairman and Chief Executive Officer of Kimco Realty Corporation

Education: BBA, accounting, City College of New York; JD, Brooklyn Law School

Career Highlights:

- Founded Kimco Realty Corporation
- In 1991, IPO ushered in the modern REIT era
- Acquired five other publicly traded REITs
- Invested in a series of failing retailers to gain control of real estate
- Built Kimco into largest shopping center (nonmall) REIT in North America

shoulder to lean on. What you can do for the troubled retailer is buy assets so it can receive cash to continue functioning. More often than not, this might entail a sale-leaseback (see Chapter 6), which lets the retailer continue to operate in specific locations. Sometimes, the retailer just needs to unload unsuccessful properties.

If the retailer pulls out of the tailspin, then you, in fact, have been of extraordinary help, and hopefully it will remember your relationship as it expands. If the retailer still falters, then you have done well because you have (1) handpicked individual assets to acquire and (2) established a relationship with the retailer for future divestitures of store sites.

Kimco undertook a series of these deals, with the brunt of them coming between 1994 and 1998.

The first major acquisition consisted of 60 retail leases that had been old Woolco stores. Founded in 1962 by Woolworth to be a big-box discounter to rival Kmart, the chain managed to limp along for 20 years before shutting down in 1983. Over the years, Woolworth found tenants for the old Woolco properties, and in 1994 Kimco bought 60 of those leases in 24 states. Today the company still manages about 37 of those properties. What was interesting in the deal is that Kimco bought only leases, not property, and negotiated downside protection. As the leases expired, Kimco had an option to give them back to the fee owner. Obviously, in some cases Kimco let the leases burn off.

In 1996, Kimco acquired 16 properties from the venerable Philadelphia department store chain Strawbridge & Clothier. As it turned out, this deal was a good one for Kimco, but not so good for Strawbridge. The company was going out of business, so it sold its Strawbridge department stores to May Department Stores and its Clover division to Kimco for $35.5 million. There were 26 Clover stores at the time, but Kimco was able to negotiate a deal whereby it would take only the 23 stores it wanted and not the whole chain.[12]

"The deal was really based on inherent real estate values," says Cooper. "We felt those 23 stores had real estate value and just needed other users."

Cooper could also tell a bad location and a bad lease when he saw one, and that was the case with the three remaining stores, which he didn't want in Kimco's portfolio. It was a brilliant decision, because years after trying to eliminate itself from the retail business, Strawbridge was still having to deal with those three stores, which hadn't found buyers.

In a very simple 2001 deal, Kimco teamed up with Simon Property Group and Schottenstein Group to acquire from bankrupt retailer

Montgomery Ward LLC all the asset designation rights (which enable the companies to direct the disposition of fee and leasehold positions held by the bankrupt estate) to its real estate. The initial price for 315 properties (250 former Montgomery Ward retail locations) was $60.5 million, but under the terms of the purchase agreement, the price could eventually end up in the $435.5 million range.[13]

Not all deals are so cut-and-dried. Kimco's most expensive retail site arbitrage was actually a series of deals done to keep the O'Fallon, Missouri–based Venture Stores Inc. on life support while it worked through financial troubles. Venture Stores eventually went out of business, but most of its properties ended up in the Kimco portfolio. In addition, during the wind down of Venture Stores, Kimco was hired to sell its "excess real estate."

In one of Kimco's first successes with the Venture real estate, it engineered a sale of 20 stores to Kmart in 1997. The establishment of the Kimco-Kmart relationship rose in importance as Venture Stores continued to teeter.

"You try to be proactive when a retailer gets on your 'watch list,' " says Cooper. "The threshold questions are whether the retailer's space can be re-leased at or above the lease rent and how essential that retailer is to the viability of the center. If it's a question of viability, sell, sell, sell. If the space is re-leasable, one must start informal marketing as soon as possible."[14]

Kimco's adventures with Venture Stores began in 1996, when it acquired 16 properties for $40 million and then leased them back to the retailer. This was followed by a second transaction the following year when Kimco acquired fee and leasehold positions in 49 more properties for $139 million.

Venture continued to lease these properties from Kimco, but then in January 1998, Venture Stores filed for Chapter 11 bankruptcy reorganization. A few months later, it finally gave up the ghost and announced it would discontinue retail operations. Instead of blanching at the prospect of holding Venture locations, Kimco plunged back into deal making, acquiring fee and leasehold rights to 89 more sites at a cost of $95 million from Venture, plus paying $167 million to Metropolitan Life, which owned 30 of the 89 locations.

Simultaneous to all that, Kimco turned around and re-leased 46 of the locations to Kmart, which the year before, as noted, had acquired 20 Venture Stores—brokered by Kimco!

Four years later, Kmart filed for Chapter 11 reorganization and began closing stores, many of which were Kimco sites. However, Kmart and Kimco knew each other well, as one stock analyst noted in 2003: "The entire Kimco and Kmart saga becomes ever more interesting. The Kmart bankruptcy is behind and Kimco has a consulting deal out of the mess."[15]

Indeed, Kimco secured an agreement with Kmart to market 317 of its properties in the United States and Puerto Rico that the retailer was closing as part of its bankruptcy reorganization.[16]

The same analyst, still writing about Kimco, added, "A good asset can be repositioned, as in changing a lease from deadbeat Kmart to expanding Target or Lowe's. Investors looking to fundamentals tend to fix on existing liabilities and assets as though they were permanent—but in a good company they are constantly being managed and improved. That is why Kimco, which sold $32.50 before the Kmart bankruptcy, now sells for over $37, and investors who followed a broker's advice to sell on the bad news have suffered."[17]

What happened was, Kmart ended up as Kimco's largest tenant, accounting for approximately 14 percent of its rental income. In 2003, Kmart closed 44 of the 70 stores it leased from Kimco locations.[18]

Kimco actually profited handsomely from the Kmart debacle. As Cooper explained to me when I interviewed him for a cover story for *Real Estate Portfolio* magazine, "We have been able to re-lease, redevelop, sell, and otherwise dispose of all but three of the 44 stores. The value of our rejection claim, which was paid in Kmart shares, became more valuable than anyone had hoped by virtue of the substantial increase in market value of Kmart stock."[19]

That was all in addition to the accord Kimco signed with Kmart to market its stores.

GETTING TO THE TOP

In recent years, anyone trying to interview Milton Cooper would have to first answer his initial question, which was always, "So, what are you reading?" The first time he popped this question to me, I was taken off guard. I recovered relatively quickly to mumble that I was thick into a volume of Jack London stories. This must have pleased him, because he gave me an immediate and quick dissertation on *White Fang* and other London books.

Actually, if I had thought about it, asking what I was reading shouldn't have been a surprise, because this was a guy who quoted Balzac in his company's 2003 annual report. You just don't see that very often.

That twinkle in his eyes? Don't let it fool you. Cooper is a hard-driving businessman, an implacable negotiator, and one hell of an out-of-the-box thinker . . . in short, a perfect maverick. If there's ever a Hall of Fame for real estate investors, Cooper would be in the inaugural group, a Honus Wagner type—not as famous as, say, a Ty Cobb or Babe Ruth, but a man of equal talent and accomplishments.

Cooper, through his four decades in real estate, built one of the great retail real estate empires in the country. Today, Kimco Realty Corporation is the largest retail (nonmall) REIT in North America, with a market capitalization as of July 2005 totaling $6.7 billion. At the end of year 2004, the company could boast ownership and management of more than 800 individual properties.

One doesn't hit those kinds of numbers by being a market wall-flower. In December 2004, a joint venture between Kimco and DRA Advisors LLC completed the acquisition of another REIT, Price Legacy Corp., for $1.2 billion. The deal brought into Kimco's fold 33 shopping centers and a parcel of undeveloped land. In a wider scheme of things, the Price Legacy transaction represented the fifth publicly traded REIT in which Kimco acquired all or most of the assets.[20]

That alone would make Cooper a Hall of Famer, but he is equally well known in the annals of real estate history as having led the way into what is sometimes called the modern REIT era.

In November 1991, Cooper took Kimco public, an act that eventually reopened Wall Street to the real estate investment trust world. After Kimco, a mad rush of REITs formed, many of which are now some of the biggest real estate companies in the world.

Up until then there had been intermittent flurries of real estate companies going public, but there was no head of steam. In 1991, there still lingered a taint from the mortgage REIT disasters of the early 1970s, and much doubt persisted about whether real estate should be held in the form of a public company. On top of all those awful trendlines, the U.S. real estate industry was still in the throes of a deep recession.

"It was a very tough time," says Cooper. "Real estate was a dirty word. Banks had almost stopped lending to real estate. There was limited capital available."

Kimco didn't escape the tough times, but Cooper knew he had a solid company, and if it could continue to grow, it would be even a better business. "We wanted nontemperamental capital," he says, "capital that wouldn't be subject to the vagaries of the market. Once you have equity in a public company, it opens up all these additional sources of capital."

To go public, companies do what is a called a "road show," trying to sell themselves as a worthwhile firm deserving of public shareholder investment. Today, Cooper is very diplomatic about that time. "It was," he says with measured pauses, "an interesting experience." What really happened was that Cooper and his real estate ilk were all but accused of single-handedly sinking the savings and loan industry—as if the S&Ls themselves didn't deserve much of that credit. "There was so much skepticism. It was very difficult," Cooper says.

Some investment bankers liked what they saw in Kimco. Cooper singles out Richard Salzman at Merrill Lynch. Other firms, such as Smith Barney and Dean Witter, signed on as well.

As Cooper told me for the *Real Estate Portfolio* article, "The institutional orders were anemic. At the last moment, one hedge fund came in with an order for 500,000 shares and this put us over the top. The underwriters and Kimco were delighted. It was only at that point we realized we were successful."[21]

He adds, "We squeaked through." The IPO was priced at $20 a share. The actual offering was for $126 million, but there was a lot of debt in the deal, so the whole transaction totaled $250 million.

Although the stock traded down immediately after the IPO, if you had invested $100,000 in the Kimco IPO, it would have been worth $1.4 million at the end 2004. (After 40 years, Cooper has never sold a single share of Kimco stock.)

Cooper is a wealthy man today, but it certainly wasn't always so. He grew up on the Lower East Side of Manhattan during the Great Depression. His father, a plumber, managed to find enough work to get the family through those very difficult years. A bright child, Cooper graduated from high school and attended City

College in New York. Afterward, he worked days and in the evenings attended classes, eventually earning a law degree from Brooklyn Law School.

Cooper's law firm handled a number of real estate clients, including Martin Kimmel, a developer of garden apartments on Long Island. They became friends. In 1958, another law firm client had a contract to build a Zayre store in Miami. When the deal blew up, Cooper talked Kimmel into helping him develop the Zayre-anchored shopping center.

"Some clients of ours and some of the partners in the law firm got together some money so the store in Florida could get built," Cooper recalls. "That's what I liked about strip shopping centers. [A strip mall] needs four times as much land as the stores, so it gets too expensive to acquire it yourself, but if you could secure a lease from a tenant, then you can easily get financing."

The Zayre center was so successful that the two men quickly moved on to a second retail project, a Winn Dixie shopping center, also in Florida. Cooper left the business of law in 1963. "The volume of activity became large enough that I couldn't do both jobs," says Cooper. "I liked real estate better than law."

Kimco (Kimmel and Cooper abbreviated) was finally and formally organized in 1966.

Today, Kimco is a much more complex company. Many of the acquisitions are done through joint ventures; the firm created a privately held, nontrading REIT called Kimco Income REIT; the company is doing business in Mexico and Canada and boasts an operating subsidiary to do ground-up development.

Kimco also established a formal unit to deal with struggling retailers. Called Retail Property Solutions, it works directly with retailers to monetize leased and fee-owned real estate through lending or sale-leaseback investments. In 2004, this unit helped a company called Frank's Nursery and Crafts, which in 2005 filed a plan for reorganization.

As Cooper notes, "Kimco intends to continue working with the reorganized company to redevelop many of its stores for alternative uses. By providing services and capital to retailers in a flexible and responsive manner, we are able to develop long-term relationships that lead to broader opportunities."

A TRUE MAVERICK'S APPROACH TO RETAIL SITE ARBITRAGE

1. To control locations of failed stores, establish relations early with the chain.
2. Opportunities arise when retailers stumble and need to reorganize on a permanent or temporary basis.
3. When considering investment opportunities based on retail sites, the key is whether those locations can easily be re-leased. Will the location be desirable to another tenant?
4. Retail site arbitrage can sometimes mean investing in the retailer to help save it. Make sure your investment is backed by the leaseholds of individual stores.
5. Sale-leaseback is a common approach to helping a retailer while at the same time securing the real estate. Some investors prefer to control the retailer first and the real estate second.
6. Joint ventures with a retailer to build shopping centers is no longer the model.
7. Does the individual store itself capture the underlying value of the real estate?
8. Retailers lease space on a long-term basis, which flattens the rental rate curve. Re-leasing to a new tenant should sharpen the curve.
9. If a single, retail chain represents a significant percentage of rental income, a useful strategy is to hedge those income sources by investing in the company. Your dollars are backed by its real estate.

10. When creditors flee, buy their bonds at discount; then you control the retailer's fate.
11. Buying a controlling interest in a failing retailer puts its real estate under your sphere of influence.
12. When buying real estate from a failing retailer, you don't have to buy it all. Negotiate for just the best properties.
13. Create ancillary income opportunities by becoming a service provider to the retailer.

CHAPTER 9

De-stressing Distressed Mortgages

A whole industry has grown up around the subject of investing in distressed real estate. The concept is very easy to understand: Buy a property that has been neglected, fix it up, and sell the gorgeously resurrected real estate at a substantial profit. The problem is, if everyone is doing the same thing, how much opportunity is left in this arena?

There is an alternative that few investors understand and that is buying up distressed real estate debt. Over the past decade and a half, fortunes have been made in this field of investing.

While researching the subject of distressed mortgages, I came across an article that I had written back in 1998 (which I didn't recall writing) about the Lehman Brothers commercial real estate unit. To show you how times have changed, the magazine then was called *Shopping Center World* and today is known as *Retail Traffic*.

What was interesting about the story was its relevance. I described what was then Lehman's Principal Transaction Group, which got its start in 1993 when it purchased $2 billion worth of distressed debt from Westinghouse for $1 billion. I then noted that the company eventually acquired more than $12 billion of distressed debt: "Most of that has already been recapitalized and repackaged into CMBS (commercial mortgage-backed securities) at a significant profit to the firm."

DISTRESSED MORTGAGES VERSUS DISTRESSED REAL ESTATE

Instead of directing my efforts to distressed real estate for this book, I decided to focus on distressed real estate debt, sometimes referred to as *distressed mortgages,* or in official parlance, *nonperforming loans,* because this is a book about real estate finance and not necessarily about real estate per se.

Second, the play on distressed real estate has been so overpublicized that an entire industry has evolved around teaching others to invest in that particular sector. Books and seminars abound; too many to track. Here's just one example of a professional group's offering: Appraisal Institute Seminars presented "Analyzing Distressed Real Estate." During the seminar, attendees reviewed basic issues that cause real estate to become distressed, explored as-is value concepts to more accurately analyze distressed real estate properties, distinguished between entrepreneurial profit and cost of capital, and reviewed adaptive use potential on distressed real estate.

Obviously, these are key issues in regard to playing in the field of distressed real estate, but the subjects are also pertinent to distressed real estate debt. Investing in distressed mortgages is a different game and not as overplayed as distressed real estate. The problem with the latter is that, because of the proliferation of seminars and books, so many novices have been scouring the countryside looking for these types of properties that the opportunities to find those distressed gems are now few and far between. About the only people making money in this field are the authors and the speakers. After all, if there is that much money still to be made in buying distressed homes, why aren't they doing it instead of giving speeches and writing books about it?

This isn't to say there aren't "issues" in regard to investing in distressed mortgages. The most important considerations are as follows: This field of investment is much more cyclical than buying up, for example, distressed homes, or even commercial properties; owners may consistently pay their mortgages while letting their properties run down; other factors such as interest rate levels weigh heavily on the distressed mortgage market.

Since the late 1990s, especially in the turn-of-the-millennium, low-interest-rate environment, the distressed mortgage market in the United States has been, shall we say, *distressed.*

A DECADE OF INVESTING IN DISTRESSED MORTGAGES

The heyday of distressed mortgage investing occurred about a decade ago in the wake of the deep real estate recession of the late

1980s and early 1990s, which was so profound it almost killed off the savings and loans, which were major real estate lenders.

In the mid-1990s, one real estate professional looked back on the previous years with these comments (condensed): "Fallout generated by the debt excess of the 1980s was not pretty. The slowing economy contributed to the decline of commercial real estate values in major metropolitan markets, volatile financial markets, the collapse or seizure of financial institutions, lower asset values, and increasingly rigorous credit evaluations.

"Many developers who previously leveraged their assets were unable to meet or refinance their existing obligations. As an alternative to foreclosure, a lender could choose to restructure the debt. The negotiations which took place between the lender and the developer explored the possibilities of restructuring the loan. The parties to the workout were acutely aware that failure to satisfy all the creditors could lead to formal bankruptcy proceedings and thereby undo the plan."[1]

Due to these widespread problems, a whole new class of investor arose in the mid-1990s to buy, not the distressed real estate, but the distressed loans. These organizations were originally called *vulture funds,* then morphed into the more politically correct *opportunity funds,* and now are known by the even more formal appellation of *private equity real estate funds.*

A University of Pennsylvania report noted, in the aftermath of the savings and loan industry's collapse, that the federal government had accumulated vast pools of nonperforming real estate loans and lesser-quality properties through the Resolution Trust Corporation (RTC). Wall Street investment firms identified an opportunity in creating funds that would buy wholesale loan pools from the RTC and either resell the underlying properties or restructure the nonperforming loans to turn a profit.

These funds differed from earlier, similar funds in that sponsors were compensated by a 1 to 2 percent fee on committed capital and an interest that is subordinated to the returns on investors' money. The sponsors didn't gain if the value of their properties didn't rise. They got the bulk of their compensation in the form of their "subordinated interest" (generally 20 percent of profits). If the funds failed to generate the promised returns, their subordinated interest was worthless paper. The other important change real estate private equity funds brought about was that along with their investors, the fund sponsors invested anywhere from 2 to 25 percent in the properties. This, along with the change in the compensation structure, opened up a more mature market for real estate entrepreneurs looking for capital.[2]

One of the first companies to organize funds to invest in distressed loans was Los Angeles–based Colony Capital Inc., now Colony Capital LLC. It began life in 1990 specifically to invest in the "distressed" marketplace and became one of the largest acquirers of nonperforming loans in the United States.

As I noted, investing in distressed mortgages is cyclical, and by the mid- to late 1990s, many of the major investors had worked through the bad loans left over from the recession and found few new opportunities in the United States. As a result, investors who wanted to continue playing in this arena moved overseas, where the market was lagging U.S. cycles.

In September 1998, as an example, an investment fund formed by Colony Capital and Kennedy Wilson bought a portfolio of 25 distressed Japanese properties and loans. The fund paid less than $40 million for the portfolio, which originally was valued at more than $400 million. At the time, the fund expected to purchase up to $350 million in Japanese real estate owned (REO) property (which goes back to the lender after an unsuccessful foreclosure auction) and nonperforming loans.[3]

A QUICK WAY TO BUY DISTRESSED PROPERTIES

The distressed real estate debt market in the United States did not totally disappear.

In 1998, the *Pacific Business News* reported on the Hawaii market with this headline: "Acquiring Property by Buying Distressed Loans Gains Popularity."

The reporter began the story by revealing the investment's ways and means. "The unconventional process of acquiring real estate by buying a troubled mortgage at a discount, foreclosing on the asset and then bidding for it at public auction is gaining popularity. . . ."

The story then turned to a Kennedy Wilson vice president who revealed a couple of key points about the investment:

- It's an attractive vehicle for investors to use and ultimately end up with real property.

- Investors look at distressed notes rather than waiting for the associated real property to hit the market through bankruptcy or lender-induced foreclosure sales.

- Buying a distressed note remains a fast way to acquire troubled property at a good savings, depending on how delinquent the note is, who the lender and borrower are, and what the asset is.[4]

After the tech bubble burst, around the year 2000, most of the commercial real estate markets, except for retail, began to underperform. Vacancy rates for office, industrial, and multifamily rose quickly, resulting in a corresponding drop in rental rates. Normally, this would result in great opportunities for distressed mortgage investors, as underperformance would eventually lead to troubled investments. Simply put, cash flow would fall below the cost of the mortgage.

However, unlike at the end of the 1980s, investors were bailed out by the Federal Reserve, which pushed interest rates down to record lows. Investors, instead of trying to get rid of troubled properties, could refinance at a lower interest rate, thereby dropping the cost of ownership. Not necessarily the best market for distressed loan investors.

ALWAYS OPPORTUNITIES

Again this doesn't mean there weren't opportunities.

In 2002, the Bascom Group LLC of Irvine, California, launched a $250 million opportunity fund to invest in distressed real estate assets. The fund's objectives were to assume control of underlying real estate assets or restructuring loans by purchasing senior and mezzanine loans.

Jerome Fink, a cofounder of Bascom duly noted, "Many borrowers have been saved by this historically low interest rate environment. However, many borrowers who locked in high-rate conduit debt in the mid- to late-1990s are suffering and cannot pay off their loans due to high defeasance (borrower voids a bond or loan by setting aside cash or bonds sufficient enough to service the debt) or prepayment costs and higher loan to value concerns."[5]

Perhaps Fink was onto something, albeit a little early, because in March 2005 the *Financial Times* reported: "Non-performing loans in the mortgage business of General Motors Acceptance Corp. (GMAC) rose from $1.3 million to $3.4 billion in 2004 as it boosted lending to subprime clients and was strong-armed into keeping more debt on its balance sheet in the post-Enron accounting era. GM officials assure that the more-than-double increase was anticipated, as the unit had deliberately accelerated its lending to poorer customers—who typically are charged a higher rate of interest."[6]

A formal reference to distressed mortgages can take either one of two phrasings: *nonperforming loans* or *REO* (real estate owned).

Generally, the process by which a loan becomes nonperforming starts when a borrower fails to make a required payment on a loan and loan officers attempt to collect the payment by contacting the borrower. If a payment on a loan has not been received by the end of a grace period (usually 10 days from the payment due date), notices are sent. If the delinquency exceeds a given time period, about 29 days, and is not cured through normal collection procedures, more formal measures are instituted to remedy the default, including the commencement of foreclosure proceedings. When the foreclosure process completes, the property is sold at a public auction in which the lender generally participates as a bidder. If the lender is successful, the acquired property is then included in a foreclosed real estate account until it is sold.[7]

"The banks have a whole series of nomenclature that goes from nonperforming loans to semiperforming loans to watch-list loans," says Thomas Barrack, chairman and chief executive officer of Los Angeles–based Colony Capital LLC. "Distress is a general category. In general investing, a nonperforming loan has a balance sheet effect—a charge to capital."

LENDERS WANT TO DIVEST TROUBLED LOANS

Why would financial institutions want to sell distressed loans? There are four good reasons why lenders want to unload this stuff:

1. *To return managerial focus and resources to core competencies.* Distressed loans consume managerial time and company resources.

2. *To redeploy capital toward areas of greater opportunity.* Sales of distressed loans empower financial organizations to redeploy resources of higher and more stable growth and greater strategic benefit.

3. *To improve ratios for rating agencies.* Underperforming assets typically increase the risk profile of financial organizations and may result in average or poor risk ratings that compromise the organizations' ability to attract capital.

4. *To create a predictable outcome for uncertain assets.* The selective sale of credit-intensive assets creates predictable outcomes and cash flow for assets that are currently uncertain.[8]

OWNING MORTGAGES IS ALL ABOUT CONTROL

Why would investors want to acquire distressed loans? One very good reason: to control the asset.

I was looking for the best way to phrase the advantages of investing in distressed mortgages when I came across a Citicorp explanation for its program of investing in distressed corporate debt. It was so good that I decided to borrow it for my own purposes. Here it is, with me exchanging a few words in the text (those in italics) to make it appropriate for our purposes.

> Distressed *mortgage* investing is often used to take control of *properties* that have either filed for bankruptcy or appear likely to do so in the near future. A major advantage of distressed *mortgage* investing is that it often allows investors to take control of *properties* at very attractive valuations. Distressed *mortgage* firms generally make their highest returns not by liquidating a *property* but by nursing it back to health. The strategy

of distressed *mortgage* firms involves first becoming a major creditor of the target *property* by buying the *property's loans* at bargain-basement prices. This gives them the leverage they need to influence the decision-making process during either the reorganization or the liquidation of the *real estate*. However, there is no guarantee that distressed investors will be able to affect a turnaround of a *property,* and this failure could lead to significant losses.[9]

One investor in nonperforming and subperforming mortgages and deeds of trust secured by single-family dwellings touted an overarching strategy to convert the distressed assets to cash as quickly as feasible to maximize the return on equity. His modus operandi is as follows: (1) Attempt to renegotiate with existing lenders. The investor keeps the basis in distressed assets low enough to offer flexibility on payoff amounts with new lenders and to ensure that transactions have a chance to close. In the event this offer doesn't prevail, then (2) negotiate with the lender (or heirs of the asset) to secure a deed-in-lieu to try to avoid the foreclosure process. If those two measures prove unsuccessful, then (3) go to foreclosure.[10] (Every state has different foreclosure procedures. To profit, investigate foreclosure methods and length of process.)

The theory behind all this is that the selected acquisition of distressed assets, especially in the form of "defaulted loans" or "bad loans," creates predictable outcomes of cash flows for assets that are currently uncertain.

Key point to keep in mind: Favorable pricing and the ability to underwrite risk and evaluate loan files and assets in advance of the acquisition substantially increase the opportunity for a successful deal.[11]

MEET THE MAVERICKS

Thomas J. Barrack

Birth Date: 1947

Occupation: Founder, Chairman, and CEO of Colony Capital LLC

Education: BA, sociology, University of Southern California; JD, University of San Diego

Career Highlights:

- Helped restructure American Savings (now Washington Mutual Inc.)
- Founded Colony Capital LLC, creator of real estate investment funds
- Created one of the first opportunity funds to deal with distressed real estate loans
- Managed one of the few real estate opportunity funds to operate overseas
- Extensively invested in and restructured lodging and casino properties

BANKS LIKE TO SELL BIG

The problem with distressed mortgages is that lenders normally don't sell just one loan; they prefer to sell a pool of loans, which is why great gobs of capital are raised. Nevertheless, it is strategy that can work for a small investor. Let's say, for example, you want to buy a house, but the owners are being unreasonable.

The situation is this, you want to buy a $2 million dollar house for $1.7 million, but you learn the owner has a $1.5 million mortgage that is in default. You can go to the lender and say, "I know the loan is in default and I will buy it from you." You are willing to pay par, that is, 100 percent of what the lender is owed. If the lender is willing to make the deal, then you, as holder of the loan, become the lender. Think of it: Suddenly, your conversation with the owner of the house takes on a whole new primacy since you are in control of the note.

Barrack likes to say that in his world there are two kinds of distressed—distressed owners and distressed assets, and the two are very different.

Approaching distressed buyers is easier because it simply means evaluating their position. What is the best formula to allow you to solve the buyer's problem? On one hand, there is a lot of flexibility in dealing with distressed owners. On the other hand, distressed assets offer many fewer options. Everything is black and white—and control of the debt is everything. There's a joke in the distressed real estate business that to buy these kinds of properties is counterintuitive. After all, how do you pat yourself on the back for being the highest bidder.

GOOD WORKS CREATES GOOD CONTACTS

Thomas Barrack's journey into real estate investing and subsequently investing in distressed loans, oddly enough, begins in the mid-1970s in Saudi Arabia, when as an attorney he helped arrange a way for a U.S. oil and gas company to transship oil from the Middle East through Haiti to the United States. Barrack did such a good job, his contact invited him to partner on a commercial real estate company back in the United States.

Barrack not only didn't know anything about real estate, but, as he says, "I never even built anything." He proved a quick learner, because the partnership's first big contract was to construct 2,000 Del Tacos around the country. "We did very well; we got everything done and sold off the leases," Barrack recalls. "We then started developing multitenant industrial and office space around the country."

In 1979, the partner retired and moved to Europe, leaving Barrack to run the company. Soon after, Barrack had an epiphany. "I realized in this whole building business that 90 percent of the money was made by 10 percent of the effort—the financing. And that 90 percent of the effort, the actual building, was responsible for only 10 percent of the profitability."

He recalls, "As I watched this stream of hundreds of millions of dollars, I could see very clearly where the beta was."

It was also during these entrepreneurial days that Barrack formed his investment philosophy, which he calls the Waldo, after the *Where's Waldo* books. The way the real estate game operates, Barrack realized, is that everyone is searching for something that is being overlooked—a building, land, or portfolio—and once it is found, the market for it quickly becomes efficient and the deals disappear.

"The Waldo books are a great example of my investment style," Barrack explains. "Everybody is looking for Waldo on the page, but no one sees him. As soon as someone spots him, the page is of no use anymore and you have to turn to the next page."

In 1979, Barrack sold his company to Oxford Properties Group Inc., a large Canadian development firm, and worked for them for a while before moving on to become deputy secretary of the Interior during the Reagan administration. The next stop was E.F. Hutton on Wall Street. Then, in the mid-1980s, he joined some of the highly regarded Texas investors involved with the Robert M. Bass Group and returned to entrepreneurial real estate. This group made two very significant and successful investments: (1) the acquisition of 62 hotels, including the famed Plaza Hotel in New York, from

Westin Hotels & Resorts (acting on behalf of the Robert M. Bass Group and John Aoki), and (2) the less-well-known, but more important, American Savings Bank in 1987.

"We started looking at this [American Savings] as a real estate deal because it had a property group that was working out all its troubled real estate," says Barrack. "This was before any of us knew what distressed debt was, what nonperforming loans were."

ARBITRAGE BETWEEN BANK AND INVESTOR VALUATIONS

American Savings was the first good bank–bad bank structure from the federal government, as it had about $15 billion in good assets and $15 billion in bad assets. Barrack's job was to take the "bad bank" and figure out what to do with $15 billion of bad assets. (The good bank of American Savings eventually morphed into Washington Mutual Inc.)

"While working with the bad loans, I discovered that this was a very good business in that there was a gigantic arbitrage between the value that a borrower really had in mind for a particular piece of property and the value the banking process put on the same property," says Barrack. "Think of it this way: Let's say American Express called you up one day and said, 'We know you are having a tough go of it these days; instead of paying me the $2,000 you owe me, why don't you pay me $1,000?' "

All this was good background, because by the year 1990, the country's real estate market was in a deep funk. The savings and loans were being shut down, and banks, life insurers, and almost everyone else stopped lending. There was no liquidity in the real estate markets.

At this point one of Barrack's partners left to buy Continental Airlines, but that was okay, because Barrack had figured out what his next step should be. First, he had all that experience with bad loans from American Savings, and second, his gut instinct told him that when everyone else was fleeing the real estate market was a good time to go in and start buying.

In 1991, Barrack formed Colony Capital Inc. and Colony I, the first of what would eventually become known as *opportunity funds.* The purpose of the funds was to produce much greater returns than those traditionally obtained in institutional real estate investment over the prior two decades. The sponsors of the funds invested their own capital alongside that of the institutional investors. This investment was true risk capital; consequently, expected returns were appropriately gauged for the unknown risks.[12]

RAISE CAPITAL IN ADVANCE TO MOVE QUICKLY

In addition, these funds were organized with a finite life. The purpose was midterm extraordinary gain and not long-term residual growth. It was never envisioned that the opportunity fund would be a continuing business, but rather what Barrack calls an "entrepreneurial response" by risk capital to a temporary mismatch of funds and product. Since capital was raised ahead of the investments, the funds had large amounts of nondiscretionary dollars to move quickly and participate in competitive auctions of large portfolios of nonperforming loans.[13]

Opportunity funds were leveraged. The Colony I fund ended up acquiring $2.5 billion worth of assets. The average holding period for assets from 1991 to 1994 was 18 months, and the average return was 70 percent.

Around the mid-1990s, all the low-hanging fruit in regard to distressed loans had been taken. The market had become so very efficient, Barrack turned his attention overseas, where real estate cycles track behind those in the United States.

The company honed its distress and restructuring skills during the real estate debacle and Resolution Trust Corporation remedies of the early 1990s. The market then was inefficient, capital was scarce, and, as Barrack noted, mispricing was plentiful. The art of rescuing and restructuring bad loans and bad banks was a cooperative effort among governmental bank regulators, accountants, Wall Street, Congress, and the newly created opportunity funds.[14] By 1995, most of the bad loan problems had been resolved and the market had become efficient again.

DISTRESSED LOAN BUYERS FOLLOW THE MARKETS

Colony Capital found itself still armed with a set of disciplines to resolve distressed real estate loans, and so it looked to markets where it could use these skills. Its first stop was Europe.

Colony first began buying nonpaying loans in Europe in 1994 and then Asia in 1997. Colony still does a lot of deals in Asia. In 2005, Barrack summed up the continent in regard to distressed mortgages, "China is exploding, Japan recycling, Korea almost through, and Taiwan had a little."

As a result of being so active overseas, Colony in 2005 could boast 14 offices in seven countries around the globe.

BETTING ON REAL ESTATE–DEPENDENT OPERATING COMPANIES

Also in the mid-1990s, Colony began investing in operating companies that are real estate–dependent, such has hotels and casinos. What Barrack saw in these companies was a nearly uncontested field. "Real estate people want no operating headaches," he explains.

"They want an A-quality site with an A-quality building and an A-quality lease that matches cash flow to debt. They never want to think about an operating piece on top of that. It makes it unattractive for them."

However, the leverage buyout pros don't like real estate, he adds. "They are buying companies at a multiple, leveraging them at another multiple, and then taking the company public at a higher multiple. The more real estate on the balance sheet, the lumpier the deal is. Real estate hurts the balance sheet."

As a result, Barrack could see opportunity in the difference. The complexity of operating companies dependent on the underlying real estate assets presented great arbitrage opportunities.

Barrack had been used to hotel deals since his early transaction with Westin. Since then, Colony has done investments in AmanResorts (mostly in Southeast Asia), Savoy Group Hotels (five deluxe hotels in the United Kingdom), CGSH Hotel Group (a deal with Accor), and such individual properties as Hyatt Regency Waikoloa (Hawaii), 610 Park Avenue (New York), The Orchid at Mauna Lani (Hawaii), Hotel Guanahani (St. Bart's), Stanhope Hotel (New York), and Resorts International Atlantic City.

The company also invested in the Punch Group, second-largest pub landlord in the United Kingdom, with more than 5,000 pubs.

Beyond hotels and pubs, the company has cut a wide swath in casinos as well. Its privatization of Harveys Casino Resorts was the first true leveraged buyout in the gaming industry in America. In the process, Colony became one of the few private equity firms to navigate the gaming regulatory and licensing processes. Harveys was successfully sold to Harrah's Entertainment in July 2001 after several additions, expansions, and operating improvements.

The company is still very active in casino plays. In 2004, Colony swung two major investments on two continents. In Europe, Colony

Capital joined with Accor, the big French hotel company, and a private investor to form Groupe Lucien Barriere, which at the time owned 37 casinos, 14 luxury hotels, and 5,000 gaming machines.

On this side of the Atlantic, the merger of Harrah's Entertainment Inc. and Caesars Entertainment Inc. meant some assets in the Midwest and East Coast had to be divested. Colony Capital LLC paid $1.24 billion for Harrah's East Chicago, Harrah's Tunica, Atlantic City Hilton, and Bally's Tunica.

"Back in 1998, we looked at Harveys and saw that its real estate assets were worth more than its stock value," Barrack recalls. "The problem was how to liquefy that investment. It needed to be sold to someone who was licensed, so we took that giant step."

It turned out to be a big advantage years later with the Harrah's/Caesars deal. There are only a handful of strategic players in the U.S. gaming industry, and they don't want to sell their divested properties to each other. They have to find another party who is licensed to buy casino assets and who can fix them up and eventually sell them again.

"Some of those regulatory agencies take two to three years to get through, so we built a multi-billion-dollar business out of the bet that we should get licensed," says Barrack. "We were there at the moment the gaming companies needed us."

What happens when a country such as the United States enters a cyclical downturn in the real estate sector? At first, during the restructuring phase, there is little or no new construction and the real estate inventory is basically repriced to market. Absorption accelerates and a recovery slowly materializes. At some point in the recovery, supply and demand curves will cross and the demand will then warrant the repositioning and redevelopment of nontroubled real estate products.[15]

In the years 1995 through 1999, the United States entered a

value-added stage that enticed billions of dollars of new capital and thousands of new entrants into the real estate market, which became very liquid, and returns retreated with the perceived lessening of associated risk.[16]

U.S. MARKET STILL VERY EFFICIENT

In the years 2002 to 2005 some companies, such as the Brascom example I mentioned earlier, felt real estate markets were moving toward a position where distressed real estate loans would again be more common and thus attract capital, but Barrack was still not finding the mispricings necessary for him to return to that market. As he saw it, the U.S. market was quite efficient and, in fact, over-heated with investment capital. While fundamentals were weak, excess capital and cheap debt shielded owners from value deflation. Still, he was keeping an eye on markets, especially hospitality, health care, and office.

Curious to see how Barrack's mind works? Here's how he intuits a typical real estate opportunity. "Leverage core products might be a sucker punch." And here's the explanation: A 9 percent cap rate on "acceptable credit" when leveraged at 65 percent loan-to-value and 5 percent interest rates produces an apparent 17 percent yield. However, this might also convert to a $350-per-square-foot purchase price in a building that has a current market price at $100 a square foot. This execution is illusory in that many of the transactions are calculated on above-market current rents. Buyers in this situation are essentially betting on the interim credit of the tenant and the hope that residual value will catch up to the values supported by the above-market rents before the expiration of the lease term.[17]

In the United States, Barrack says, "Everyone is working on a very level playing field and it is hard to find the edge at the moment. The next edge may be the cliff."[18]

This is bad for initial investors, but good for companies such as Colony Capital that can come in, buy into the mess, get the real estate financially and operationally scrubbed, and put it back on the market. "Our U.S. motto is," says Barrack, "if bad is good, worse is better."[19]

A TRUE MAVERICK'S APPROACH TO DISTRESSED MORTGAGES

1. Investing in distressed real estate loans is an alternative to investing in distressed real estate.
2. Distressed real estate investing is overplayed.
3. Distressed mortgages offer high returns.
4. Investing in distressed loans is a fast way to acquire troubled properties.
5. While the market for distressed loans remains cyclical, opportunities can arise even in good times.
6. Financial institutions want to get rid of distressed loans.
7. If you control the mortgage, you control the property.
8. Banks prefer to sell troubled loans in bulk, but individual deals work.
9. Best play: Buy loans and nurse properties back to health.

CHAPTER 10

Commingled Capital

Limited partnerships have always been the basic legal structure by which numerous investors pool capital to make investments beyond each individual's financial capability. Despite a troubled history due to the collapse of tax-shelter-driven syndications, the limited partnership remains an efficient and effective real estate investment format.

When I arrived in Chicago to do two interviews for this book, my wife and I were met at the airport by her aunt and uncle, who were taking us to their house in Highland Park, where we would be staying. When I explained why we had come to Chicago, my wife's aunt asked if I would be interviewing anyone from JMB Realty, as they knew two of the principals who had formed that pioneering real estate venture back in the 1960s.

Actually, I explained, one of the companies I would be visiting was called Heitman, a real estate investment management firm that in 1994 acquired the institutional management and property management components of JMB Realty.

That long-ago connection puts Heitman in this chapter on limited partnerships. If you, as the reader, discern a pattern in my books, it's that the chapter subject usually has an integral relationship to the company I profile in that particular chapter. That's not quite the case here. Heitman, which sponsors a number of pooled real estate investment vehicles called *commingled funds,* doesn't create retail-oriented limited partnerships; the company it raided a decade back did. It's all ancient history now, but in the decade and a half, from roughly 1970 through 1986, when the tax law changed, limited partnerships ruled the real estate investment roost. And JMB Realty ruled the limited partnership world.

Limited partnerships never went away. In fact, a number of maverick financiers, such as Leo Wells of Wells Real Estate Funds and W. P. Carey of W.P. Carey & Company LLC, have been offering limited partnerships for decades. The structure was always sound, which is why limited partnerships have been making a strong comeback since the turn of the millennium.

Here's an interesting statistic from Robert A. Stanger & Co., a

Shrewsbury, New Jersey–based research firm specializing in limited partnerships: In 2003, $7 billion worth of partnership units were sold. That compared with $8 billion in shares of publicly traded REITs. Just five years before, the ratio was 4 to 1 in favor of REITs.[1]

When the limited partnership industry began to fall apart in the late 1980s, it was due to the fact limited partnerships were originally constructed as tax shelters, using accelerated depreciation. The Tax Reform Act of 1986 did two things in regard to limited partnerships: (1) It eliminated accelerated depreciation, and (2) it eliminated the leniency of the passive loss. Prior to the act, wealthy investors could use those passive losses to shelter any kind of income, earned or unearned. After the act, passive losses could shelter only passive income.[2]

However, limited partnerships that weren't designed as tax shelters continued to perform well for investors. Even today, there are some tax considerations in regard to the investment.

PRIMARY POOLS

I always considered the limited partnership one of the basics of real estate investment, mostly because of its versatility—a group of people can get together and pool their capital to create a bigger portfolio of real estate than they could have envisioned on their own.

Individuals aren't the only ones who would want to do this. Big institutional investors like pension funds pool capital as well, usually through commingled funds (collective investments of pension fund assets) such as the ones Heitman sponsors. Like retail investors, institutions have a number of options when it comes to how they hold title to their investments, including limited partnerships and limited liability companies.

Anyone interested in real estate investing eventually comes across the possibilities of forming a limited partnership or investing in an existing one or in one being formed.

In the beginning of the planning process to form a limited partnership, the major consideration is usually about the number of investors the sponsor intends to solicit. In most cases, a syndication will consist of 10 to 50 members, often known personally to the sponsor, who is probably a real estate broker, an attorney, an accountant, or someone fully involved in real estate investing. In these cases, no elaborate marketing plan needs to be implemented. In addition, federal securities laws may not apply if the offering is within a single state or otherwise meets the requirement for redemption.[3]

When considering a limited partnership investment, you'll encounter a lot of familiar terms defined in ways you might not be used to. These phrases or words are tossed about so much that they tend to lose their reference points. However, a real estate limited partnership, often referred to by its acronym RELP, is a legal entity, and therefore terms have specific meanings.

Two words formed from the same root that any limited partnership investor frequently encounters are *syndicator* and *syndications.*

- *Syndicator.* A person who sells equity interests in real estate (REIT, limited partnership, or corporation) to investors; the organizer or operator of a syndication; the catalyst who brings investors together and has the expertise to structure the syndication and supervise the operation. The syndicator usually becomes the general partner, and any internal syndication agreement between the GP and the limited partners (investors) must cover a variety of items of potential conflict. Some typical items covered are fees and benefits paid to or obtained by the syndicator; the apportionment of cash flows, taxable income (losses), and reversion proceeds; management control and costs; the apportionment of present and future equity requirements; provisions for removal of uncooperative partners; and buy-sell procedures.[4]

- *Syndication.* While the syndication may take corporate or general partnership forms of ownership, the preferred structure is the limited partnership, which provides limited liability for the limited partners and places the responsibility for operation on the general partner (syndicator). It is not a taxable entity like the corporation, so cash flows and tax benefits flow through directly to the individual investors in a limited partnership.[5]

- *Formation.* Syndicators, or the limited partnership promoters, can approach syndication by first acquiring a property interest and then seeking investors. This methodology is called a *specific asset syndication,* whereby the syndicator may control a property through a purchase option or outright ownership. If a syndicator starts with a pool of investors and then seeks an appropriate property, it is known as a *blind pool syndication.* With the specific asset syndication, investors have an opportunity to evaluate properties and their promoters, but in the latter instance, investors who put funds into a blind pool have only the promoter's track record to guide them.[6]

WHAT IS IT?

The problems with the first generation of limited partnerships, the ones from the 1970s and early 1980s, can be attributed to the fact that these pools of capital were in many cases set up only as tax shelters, and absent those tax incentives they weren't investment-driven through economic returns.

Companies like JMB Realty made the tax syndication aspects of limited partnerships very attractive, avers Maury Tognarelli, president and chief executive officer of Heitman. "The bad news was a lot of real estate limited partnerships were created that never should have been created. When the tax laws changed in 1986, the investors realized the economics they needed in order to achieve some return on capital were not there. What they ended up with was a significantly poor-performing investment."

The whole limited partnership industry ended up with a bad name. While a lot of the business dried up, a number of firms stayed the course. There was very little publicity about the investment structures—as though they had gone underground. When the financial press happened upon them, it was always a surprise.

In a 1991 article in the *Journal of Accountancy,* an author wrote, "Rumors of the death of tax shelters may be greatly exaggerated." In 1996, *Business Week* offered "back from the dead: limited partnerships. In 2003, the *Dallas Business Journal* reported, "One investment bastion in the 1970s—the real estate limited partnership—is returning to popularity." And in 2004, *Investor's Business Daily* observed, "A once popular investment is seeing its days in the sun again in a different climate. Riding the wave of investor interest in real estate, limited partnership units are making a comeback."

Limited partnerships apparently are the Energizer Bunny of the real estate world. While not all are created equal, they do all share common attributes. As I mentioned, the words *limited partnership* do not constitute something general, but something specific. Here are some key features.

• *General and limited partners.* All limited partnerships must have at least one general partner and one or more limited partners. General partners have operational control and bear unlimited liability for partnership obligations. Limited partners receive all the investment benefits that typically accrue and may reap additional advantages resulting from choosing this investment path.[7]

- *Regulation.* Limited partnership shares are considered securities just as are corporate stocks and bonds. As securities, they are potentially subject to both federal and state securities laws. If required to register offerings with the Securities and Exchange Commission, syndicators must file a preliminary prospectus prior to advertising and have it approved before sale. RELPs may claim exemption from registration if the partnership is a private placement or an intrastate offering.[8]

- *Documentation.* (1) Prospectus or offering memorandum that fully discloses nature of the offering; (2) partnership agreement that defines the relationship between general and limited partners; (3) subscription agreement to be signed; and (4) questionnaire if the RELP is a private placement or intrastate offering.[9]

- *Pro rata.* In a typical syndication, the investors constitute a single class, each receiving a pro rata ownership interest in the syndicate. In order to broaden the market for shares, the sponsor can create multiclass syndicates or paired syndicates.[10]

A BETTER PRODUCT

There was a point in time, at least through the early 1990s, when investors were dissatisfied with the results from real estate, Tognarelli recalls. The real estate markets were underperforming, and investors needed to get information, but it was hard to get. "Market data at the time was fragmented, and this resulted in mixed information and local interpretation challenges. Investment information was available, but without good market intelligence, it made it difficult for investors to make informed decisions," says Tognarelli.

He adds, "Investment performance was less than expected, liquidity was less than expected, the transparency needed to make educated decisions was not there, and there was no alignment of interest between the investment managers and client."

While most of those problems have been eliminated, from an investor's standpoint some inherent problems still remain. There's a lot more transparency today about the individual assets in each partnership, but when a large pool of capital is raised that subsequently acquires a substantially diverse portfolio of properties, it's difficult to grasp the value of each asset. In addition, investors are sometimes asked to participate in a limited partnership where the assets have not yet been designated.

Again, from an investor's standpoint, the liquidity problem with limited partnerships hasn't changed much. They are still difficult and expensive to exit.

In the old days, a general partner could still make a lot of money due to fees from the limited partnership, even if the investments themselves were losing money. Nowadays, investors want the general partner to have capital in the limited partnership so that if it goes down, the general partner suffers as well. That's called aligning the interests of the general partner and limited partners.

Nevertheless, since the general partner operates as kind of a fund manager, he or she plays a huge role in the investment's success or failure. Potential investors should consider these factors when selecting a general partner: (1) The GP should be experienced in the type of real estate involved, have extensive knowledge of local factors, and carry a sound track record of operating buildings and making money for investors; (2) the GP should actively participate in the property's management direction and stay in communication with the tenants; and (3) investors should carefully examine the partner's financial prospectus and reporting, know if cash flow budgets are realistic and analyze budget projections.[11]

In the old days, general partners got a bad rap—and for good reason. Many put their fee-raking motives before the interests of their limited partnerships. General partners have complete control, so it's best to stick with partners who have good, well-known management and investment track records. A prospectus should report accurate results. Also, look for partnerships in which sponsors sold to their own clients, such as big brokerage firms and insurance companies.[12]

GOOD BUSINESS

Why form a limited partnership? The simple answer is because bigger is sometimes better. A real estate syndication such as the limited partnership is put together by a group of like-minded investors who commingle their investment capital, thus giving them the ability to acquire a bigger or more diverse or higher-quality investments than they could using just their own devices—and capital.

In the summer of 2003, the accounting firm BDO Seidman LLP caught up to the rising tide of real estate aggregations and offered what I deemed to be the best summation on why limited partnerships are advantageous. My abbreviated and reconstituted version of the BDO Seidman list looks like this:

- *Investment knowledge.* For a nonprofessional investor, investing with a syndication means access to the required skills in determining real estate values, negotiating purchase agreements, financing, lease negotiations, and property management.

- *Less outlay.* For an individual investor, a good-sized investment takes a lot of capital, but a well-capitalized syndication can make a substantial downpayment, not just on one property but on many, while still retaining cash reserves. Something to think about: Larger properties tend to be more cost-efficient than smaller ones, since many expenses are lower on a per-unit or square-foot basis.

- *Diversification.* For an investor with limited funds, a syndication offers the opportunity to diversify an investment among a number of different properties.

- *Customization.* A syndication can be structured to offer a variety of investment positions with regard to return priority, loss risk, or tax benefit. Although not a unique quality, syndications can invest in a wide range of assets or just specific types of real estate such as office buildings. Also, investors may choose the balance between risk and return that suits them best.

- *Cash reserves.* Inexperienced real estate investors are often tripped up in their investments because they retain no cash reserves. The syndication should always have sufficient capital available to give the investment the ability to withstand economic downturns or temporary operating shortfalls.[13]

- *Returns.* Compared to the more common aggregation, the REIT, the limited partnership boasts a higher dividend rate. For many investors, an income-oriented investment like the limited partnership is preferable to capital appreciation investment. (Income is the defined amount of capital returned to investors per year, compared to appreciation or rise in asset price.) Partnerships appreciate slowly, but pay investors a high dividend in return.[14]

- *Liability.* The liability of a limited partner is limited to his or her investment. In this respect, limited partners are similar to corporate shareholders.[15]

BETTER TO BE A GENERAL

As a novice real estate investor, coming into a limited partnership opportunity is often a good deal. Other people do the work, and you benefit from their skills. Hopefully, they have real estate knowledge

MEET THE MAVERICKS

Maury R. Tognarelli

Birth Date: 1961

Occupation: President and Chief Executive Officer of Heitman

Education: BS, real estate, Indiana University

Career Highlights:

- Helped merge Heitman and JMB Institutional Realty Corp./JMB Property Co.
- In postacquisition period, headed disposition of unneeded assets
- Divested property management unit
- Expanded the company's international and public securities efforts
- Reorganized Heitman management and ownership structure

and organization skills; otherwise the investment may not end up to be so great.

If, on the other hand, you are an experienced real estate investor and don't mind handling the responsibilities of putting your money and your friend's and family's capital to work, then being a general partner should be a better position. A successful limited partnership investment usually begets another limited partnership, because the word gets out when you are good. Historically, general partners in real estate limited partnerships have done very well for themselves over the years.

Although it was another time, another place, and a different economy, the best example of general partners attaining the golden gauntlet can be found in the tale of JMB Realty before it slowly dissolved into nothingness.

The high-flying JMB Realty Corporation was founded in 1969 by two University of Illinois roommates, Neil Bluhm and Judd Malkin. By persuading investors to pool their hard-earned dollars and seek tax shelters in real estate syndications, the duo undertook what the local Chicago press called "one of the great shopping sprees of all time." Before the smoke had cleared, the JMB Realty portfolio was worth 20 times the portfolio of the Trump Organization. As a result, Bluhm and Malkin became two of the richest people in the United States, each with a net worth of $500 million.

After changes in tax laws and the subsequent real estate recession, JMB had to give back some of its properties to lenders.[16] Nevertheless, Bluhm and Malkin saw a partial way out with the rise of the REIT market. In 1993, they placed their best retail properties into a portfolio and took it all public as Urban Shopping Centers Inc. For a long time, Bluhm and Malkin kept control of the company as cochairmen, but in 2000 it was acquired by Rodamco North America NV, which in turned was bought out in a messy takeover by three shopping mall heavyweights, Westfield America Trust, Simon Property Group, and The Rouse Company.

One year after the formation of Urban Shopping Centers, what was then called Heitman Financial Ltd. acquired JMB's institutional asset management and nonretail property management businesses.

A LONG DEVELOPMENT

Heitman was formed in 1966 with an early focus on mortgage banking and servicing. What the company was trying to do at the time was find a way to capitalize real estate development activity, and back in the 1960s mortgage banking was one of the few ways of doing that. The modern equity market had not yet developed, and few institutional investors were making equity investments in real estate.

By the 1970s, Heitman started to migrate into equity investment management, a complement to what it was doing on the debt side. "It was the principal's view that the marketplace for equity investment in real estate was going to flourish and institutional capital would begin to make its way into the marketplace," explains Tognarelli. "The institutions would need professional investment managers in order to help them identify those opportunities and to invest in the opportunities. Heitman had the resources, the organizational strength and the market presence to provide those services. It was a natural extension of what we were doing on the debt side."

The institutional investors that began to dabble in real estate included some very big organizations in terms of investment capital—in particular, corporate pension plans and state public retirement systems. These were large investors that could create their own diversified portfolios. However, not all pension plans and retirement systems were of such bulk; therefore, it was necessary to create commingled funds to allow a group of such investors to pool their capital.

By the 1980s, Heitman began forming commingled funds. It was a product the market needed, especially as real estate became another avenue of investment. The company reached out to smaller institutional investors wanting to take advantage of real estate investment opportunities that exceeded their own capital capabilities. Between 1980 and 1993, Heitman managed 19 commingled funds, investing in assets valued at more than $6 billion. (Prior to its acquisition of JMB's institutional asset management business in 1994, Heitman raised six funds; JMB raised 13 funds. The combined results add up to 19.)

Also in the late 1980s, the investment management business was broadened when Heitman, on behalf of its clients, began making investments in public securities of REITs.

JMB Realty, founded just a couple of years after Heitman, was on a parallel track in the 1980s. The two companies had a lot in common. Both were based in Chicago and targeted the institutional investor capital bases for making investments in real estate. There were also key differences. Heitman was strong in mortgage banking and property management, while JMB Realty used its own capital for development, principally of shopping centers. And, of course, JMB Realty was heavily involved in the creation of limited partnerships.

IMMIGRATION SUCCESS

Back in 1957, the Tognarelli family moved from Italy to the United States. The change of continents didn't slow down family expansion, and whenever a new child came along the family would move to a bigger house, but they wouldn't sell their old place, preferring to keep it as a rental. Since the family had five children, in this unusual way the Tognarellis were able to accumulate a small portfolio of rental properties.

Maury Tognarelli, who came along in 1961, remembers the not-so-joyful move from house to house, but he does have happy memories of the family taking care of its rental properties throughout the North Shore of Chicago.

After four years at Indiana University, Tognarelli got a job as a summer associate for a local company called Heitman. He never left.

In 1992, Tognarelli became head of the company's U.S. private real estate equity acquisition department, which had offices in Chicago, Los Angeles, and Minneapolis. (Since that time, he has overseen the acquisition of more than $9.2 billion worth of real estate on behalf of Heitman clients.) He was also part of the team that analyzed whether it made sense to merge Heitman with JMB Realty. After that deal happened, Tognarelli took on the added responsibilities of not only being in charge of the new investments but of disposition activity as well.

In 1994, Tognarelli began serving on the company's management, compensation, and executive committees, a precursor to being promoted to president and chief operating officer for the organization in 1999. Today, he is president and chief executive officer and a member of the firm's board of managers.

"When we made the JMB Realty deal, we acquired a portion of their business that mostly mirrored things Heitman was about," Tognarelli points out. "We acquired their institutional investment management business, and with that came $6 billion in assets and the property management and leasing functions. We took the commingled funds that they raised, their separate account relationships, and human resources that were involved in those businesses."

When the dust settled, Heitman, which had $6 billion in assets in 1994, doubled in size to having $12 billion in assets. Today, the company's assets under management total $13 billion, but the company is a much different organization now than it was then.

GLOBAL AND BROAD-BASED

Today, Heitman should be considered a broad-based real estate investment management firm that serves a global client base. The company deals with U.S. and international institutions such as pension plans, endowments, foundations, and even individual investors. Its core services include U.S. and European private real estate equity, U.S. debt, and U.S. public real estate securities.

Heitman ranks (by assets under management) eleventh among U.S. real estate investment management firms. What makes the ranking interesting is that the companies ahead of it are the usual household names: JP Morgan Chase, Morgan Stanley, Principal Financial, and so on. "Heitman kept its independence primarily because we felt it was important," says Tognarelli. "We never wanted to become part of a larger organization; we thought it would diffuse the entrepreneurial culture that exists."

At first Heitman provided a panoply of services to institutional investors wanting to invest directly in the United States, including investment management, portfolio analysis, acquisition and disposition, and asset and portfolio management, as well as investment opportunities through separate accounts or commingled funds. As early as 1995, the company began looking at opportunities in Central Europe. As a result it expanded its London office and opened another in Warsaw. In 2000, Heitman formed a commingled fund consisting of U.S., Asian, and European investors seeking investments in Central Europe.

As an example of Heitman's interest in Central Europe, the company in 2004 inked the largest real estate deal to occur in Slovakia, paying $120 million for two existing office buildings and another under development, totaling roughly 650,000 square feet. Also that year, Heitman spent $121 million to buy three additional Central European industrial portfolios, including the 550,000-square-foot Zeran Park in Warsaw, Poland.[17]

Of course, Heitman still puts together commingled funds. In January 2005, Heitman completed the closing on a commingled fund focusing on investing in joint ventures with public and private real estate operating companies in the United States. Called Heitman Value Partners LP, it harvested $400 million from 18 investors, combining large players like the California State Teachers' Retirement System with smaller investors. "Joint ventures have been our focus [with separate-account clients] for nearly a decade," Heitman executive vice president Lewis Ingall told the financial press at the time, "but there are a number of smaller [investors in the fund] who would not do it directly on their own." The fund quickly made three investments: a $250 million commitment to invest with Lillibridge Health Trust in on-campus medical office buildings, including 14 buildings already purchased; a $114 million purchase, with Storage USA, of 21 storage facilities totaling 1.5 million square feet; and a $200 million commitment to invest in development and acquisition of industrial properties in the Los Angeles and Chicago areas and parts of Texas with privately owned Ridge Properties Trust.[18]

Under Tognarelli's stewardship, Heitman has continually expanded its focus in Europe and even into Asia.

"We broadened our resources in Europe and on the public securities side, and now we are trying to diversify revenue sources," says Tognarelli. The company now counts four commingled funds in Europe and is in the process of launching a fifth (Heitman Value Partners LP). Four of the commingled funds are making direct investments in Europe, and Value Partners will be investing in the United States.

"Today, we are raising capital from the United States, Europe, Middle East, and Japan; 10 years ago our capital base was primarily in the United States," says Tognarelli. "We have diversified our assets under management. We make investments in the public and private markets in the United States and Europe in both debt and equity; 10 years ago it was debt or equity solely in the United States. The organization has changed in order to adapt to what the real estate industry is today, a global marketplace."

Forty years ago, the original Heitman focused on mortgage banking. It's still an important part of the company's operations. The company originates real estate mortgage loans for commercial developments throughout the country, plus provides servicing of these loans for institutional investors, insurance companies, and other financial institutions. As of the end of 2004, Heitman's debt group held $2.4 billion in assets under management. Its mortgages range in size from $2 million to $250 million. From 2000 through 2004, the company originated more than $3 billion in loans, with annual volume averaging $600 million. Its mortgage loan closing and servicing group oversees a portfolio of 141 commercial properties in 27 markets across the United States.

Heitman steadfastly remains globally oriented in a number of ways. First, it runs offices in London, Luxembourg, Frankfurt, Warsaw, and Tokyo. Second, the company is 50 percent owned by Old Mutual PLC, a London-listed international financial services firm.

"Old Mutual is of South African origins," explains Tognarelli. "In the late 1990s, in order to diversify outside of South Africa, they demutualized and listed as a public company in the United Kingdom. In 2000, Old Mutual acquired a U.S. company called United Asset Management Corporation, which owned an interest in Heitman. That's how they became our financial partner."

NEW STRUCTURE

Since becoming president, Tognarelli has put his stamp on the Heitman organization in a number of ways.

Structurally, his most important move was leading the divestiture of company businesses. When Heitman closed the JMB acquisition, one of the key components of the deal was the nonretail property management business of JMB Properties Co. That company was merged into Heitman Properties Ltd. With that added business, Heitman owned a hefty presence in third-party property management. The business, however, was not strategic from an organizational standpoint.

"It did not make a lot of sense to have that resource and service available to clients," says Tognarelli. "The business had changed in the United States and there were ways to access that resource that were far more economical, ways to access equally if not more talented people, and ways to better access and distribute information, data, and management tools. New technology made it so that we didn't require an in-house capbility."

He added that by outsourcing property management and leasing, the company could focus on decisions based solely on maximizing the investment's results.

Perhaps nothing was more difficult for Tognarelli than changing the ownership structure of the company. He wanted to reorganize the firm to create an ownership and decision-making organizational structure for the new millennium. "When I was brought into the governance of the organization, we had come to be a company controlled by a small subset of the senior managers," he says. "It was an organizational structure I was familiar with but not necessarily the right one to take advantage of the creativity of personnel, motivating them or allowing the company to grow effectively."

The negotiations were complicated and took months, not only with the company's financial partner but with the first-generation founders of the firm who were effectively being transitioned and succeeded by the next evolution of the organization. "We went from having no ownership to what I feel is the right amount of ownership interest in the firm," Tognarelli adds. "I helped create a new group of management personnel that could share in the decision making."

Companies such as Heitman need to offer options to investors, says Tognarelli, because different structures, goals, length of investment time, and liquidity appeal to different types of investors. "It really depends on the individual investors and how they desire to access the investment," he says.

The difference between today and the past, when companies like

JMB Realty flourished, he adds, is the amount of data now available. "The way public markets have evolved over the last 10 years has promoted quite a bit of transparency at the property level. A lot of information goes through analysis, especially how the real estate is performing."

Hopefully, whether investing in a limited partnership or just a limited liability company, all that available information will make us smarter investors.

A TRUE MAVERICK'S APPROACH TO LIMITED PARTNERSHIPS

1. There are inherent tax considerations in limited partnerships; tax benefits flow through directly to individual investors.
2. In the planning process, the number of investors is a major consideration.
3. The real estate limited partnership is a legal entity.
4. The syndicator, or promoter, usually becomes the general partner.
5. Any syndication agreement between the general partner (GP) and the limited partners must cover a variety of items of potential conflict, such as fees and benefits paid to or obtained by the syndicator.
6. The preferred syndication structure is still the limited partnership.
7. Limited partnerships provide limited liability for the limited partners.
8. All limited partnerships must have at least one general partner and one or more limited partners.
9. General partners have operational control and bear unlimited liability for partnership obligations.
10. Limited partnership shares are considered securities.
11. As securities, limited partnerships are potentially subject to both federal and state securities laws.
12. Limited partnerships are difficult and expensive to exit.
13. The general partner should be experienced in the type of real estate targeted by the limited partnership and have a sound real estate track record.
14. Limited partnerships boast a higher dividend rate than REITs.

CHAPTER 11

Of REITs and UPREITs

While real estate investment trusts were
created to provide investors with a vehicle to
participate in large property investments,
they are equally beneficial to the companies
that decide to become REITs. Besides
better tax treatment, the REIT structure
offers aggregators of property such benefits
as liquidity (the ability to move in and out of
investments quickly) and exposure to Wall
Street and its varied forms of capital. REITs
owning a portfolio of properties valued at
more than a billion dollars are no longer
unusual.

Bernardo Property Advisors Inc. was a relatively small real estate company when, in April 2004, it reorganized as a Maryland corporation called BioMed Realty Trust. Five months later, BioMed, after a successful initial public offering (IPO), was reconstituted once again as a publicly traded real estate investment trust.

On a very basic level, REITs are companies that own, and in most cases operate, income-producing real estate.[1] That would include most types of real estate organizations, including partnerships, which simply means there are host regulations that must be met before a company qualifies as a REIT. The most apparent of these requires the REIT to distribute at least 90 percent of its taxable income to shareholders annually in the form of dividends. Most REITs are publicly traded, although some varieties are private.

The first few years of the new millennium were busy ones for companies hot to become REITs. Formations of REITs tend to come in waves, and the last big wash of new REITs happened in the mid-1990s. Most of the big REITs of today, including Equity Office Properties, valued at $12.2 billion, and Simon Properties Inc., valued at $13.7 billion, went public during those years.

The current generation of REITs, which includes BioMed, are hoping to be treated equally as well by market forces.

Some real estate companies go public, meaning, of course, their shares will be traded on the open markets and investors of one type or another can own both "a piece of the Rock," better known as Prudential Financial Inc., or the Newark, New Jersey, office building that harbors the Rock. However, majority owners of some real estate companies tend not to like the restrictions inherent in being a public company, the restraints on corporate movement, and the incredible amount of financial reporting that has to be accomplished. In such cases, after a brief period of trading on the New York Stock Exchange, they go back to being privately held.

Until 2005, those were rare stories. Once public, the ambitious companies continue to grow—sometimes far beyond the wildest dreams of the company founders.

POSITIVE ATTRIBUTES

The REIT structure works well. For those investors who dream of accumulating a large portfolio of properties, the reasons REITs have proven popular are numerable. The ownership shares become valued by the public market, which often makes instant millionaires of the property owners. Plus, ownership is now liquid, because shares are traded.

In the initial public offering, the founding members of the company often retain a large portion of ownership. If the company sells 30 million shares at $20 apiece, and the founders retain a 5 percent ownership, that means the founders are about $30 million richer, just by the value of the retained shares. If you as owner want to leave the business, it's not a matter of the lengthy process involved in finding a buyer and negotiating a sale of the individual real estate. Instead, you put your shares on the open market.

Now let's take a look at the BioMed IPO. The company sold 31,050,000 shares of common stock at $15.00 per share, resulting in gross proceeds of $465.8 million.[2] That's a lot of value for a company that owned less than 10 properties when it priced its IPO.

There's another reason why companies go public: It becomes easier to access a wider range of capital sources, such as those that inhabit a place called Wall Street. Again using BioMed as an example, when it went public, it simultaneously obtained a $100 million revolving, unsecured credit facility, which the company then used mostly to finance other acquisitions.[3]

Bernardo Property Advisors was probably a pleasant small real estate firm, but as publicly traded BioMed, it could do a lot more. From August 11, 2004, when the company began trading, to September 30, it completed the acquisition of 13 properties. During the fourth quarter of 2004, the company picked up four more properties on the East and West Coasts. By year-end, BioMed's portfolio totaled 17 properties with an aggregate of 2.6 million rentable square feet.[4]

ENHANCE THE INTANGIBLES

There are other intangibles to becoming a successful REIT. If your concept is good but your company has yet to make money, or your company has been very successful in the long-run but has seen a few tumultuous years, it doesn't mean that Wall Street won't be helpful on that IPO.

In that first wave of REIT IPOs at the beginning of the 1990s, especially those at the head of the rush, there were a lot of companies running in the red. In fact, the reason owners leaped at the chance to become a REIT was to be bailed out of their problems. Remember, there was a serious real estate recession that began in the late 1980s and continued to tumble into the 1990s. A number of very successful real estate investors found themselves facing dire financial straits.

Sam Zell, one of the best-known real estate investors in the world, took different companies public in the 1990s: Equity Office Properties Inc., Equity Residential, and Manufactured Home Communities Inc. Looking back, he noted, "In the early 1990s, the commercial real estate market faced the greatest peril in its history. The industry was overleveraged, underoccupied, and bleeding cash. Its traditional sources of capital were out of business. By turning to the public markets for the first time, an industry comprising 15 percent of the nation's economy was forced to change radically and begin an equitization effort—a process that took public equity from $6 billion to $150 billion in less than 10 years."[5]

Zell can wax rhapsodic about real estate. After all, in Equity Office and Equity Residential, he created two of the biggest REITs. Zell believes size matters and that attaining larger capitalization through a REIT structure is the only way as a real estate owner-investor you can gain protection when the real estate market shifts downward, leveraging your heft to secure cheaper financing and cheaper services.

"For REITs," Zell wrote, "the freshly raised capital provided the funds for growth and the opportunity to create companies with portfolios of a size and scope never seen before. Size allowed REITs to take advantage of economies of scale in contracting for goods and services as well as providing national tenants with one-stop shopping for office and mall space and other corporate housing."[6]

The intangibles in regard to transforming your company into a REIT are that if the market likes what you are doing, then your stock will increase in price, creating even more wealth. Nothing wrong with that, right?

The year prior to BioMed going public and essentially belonging to the same graduating class was another REIT, First Potomac Realty, a Bethesda, Maryland–based owner and operator of industrial and flex properties.

The company raised $118 million in its IPO, but even better, by the end of its first financial quarter as a public company it could report that its share rose 25 percent.[7]

It, too, was not a huge company, but because of the monies gained from the IPO, it went out and spent $60 million on new properties. By the end of that first quarter as a public company, it could report owning 34 buildings on 15 properties and 2.5 million square feet of leased space.[8]

As Doug Donatelli, the company's president and chief executive officer, told the local press at the time of that first offering, the IPO not only gave the company cash to pay down debt and buy properties, it also raised the company's stature. "We feel that as a public company and with the high profile that we have today . . . we're able to source more deals than we were able to at this time last year."[9]

DOWNSIDE AND A DOWN MARKET

On the other side of the coin, if the market doesn't like your company very much, the stock price can fall, sometimes quickly, and that can certainly be deleterious to one's personal wealth.

How bad can that risk be?

According to the *Wall Street Journal*'s RealEstateJournal.com, the 19 REITS that went public in the period 2002 to 2004 underperformed, as a group with the average total return for all REITs dropping by 10 percent and underperforming the average return for REITs in the respective property sector by nearly 9 percent.

Parsing the numbers a bit more, of those 19 companies only 3 outperformed the average return for REITS and sector peers: First Potomac Realty Trust, BioMed Realty Trust Inc., and U-Store-It Trust, a Cleveland self-storage company.[10]

Let's assume all that hasn't scared you away. You're sitting there with either a grand concept and a few good properties, or a typical concept and a nice aggregation of real estate, and you want to take it all and transform your company into a REIT. Well, there's a heckuva lot to consider.

Let's start with the basics.

Up until 1960, the formation of REITs would have been ineffective, because such an investment would have been taxed twice, first at the corporate level and then at the investment level. That all changed in 1960, when the Eisenhower administration passed the Real Estate Investment Trust Act provision. Growth of the sector was relatively slow until 1986, when the Tax Reform Act of that year allowed REITs to manage their properties directly. The last key date in the history of REITs was 1992, when the first umbrella partnership REIT, or UPREIT, was formed—but more on that later.

ORGANIZATION

Checking in with the National Association of Real Estate Investment Trusts (NAREIT), the Washington, D.C., trade association for the industry, reveals a number of key points in regard to the organization of REITs.

- A REIT must be formed in one of the 50 states or the District of Columbia as an entity taxable for federal purposes as a corporation.

- It must be governed by directors or trustees.

- Its shares must be transferable.

- Beginning with its second taxable year, a REIT must meet two ownership tests. First, it must have at least 100 different shareholders. Second, five or fewer individuals cannot own more than 50 percent of the value of the REIT during the last half of its taxable year.

NAREIT makes two salient observations in regard to ownership. The first is that the REIT structure is not a good choice for closely held family businesses. This is not to say a number of families do not continue to control REITs well into the second generation of family members. A look at the shopping mall sector shows that sons of the founders are running REITs such as Simon Property Group, General Growth Properties Inc., and Taubman Centers Inc.

Second, because of the need to have 100 shareholders and the complexity of ownership percentage, it is strongly recommended to seek general legal, tax, and securities law advice prior to beginning the process of forming a REIT. In other words, a few good lawyers on your team would be very helpful. REIT formation is complex, and the process takes a considerable investment. This is not something to be planned on a napkin while meeting with a couple of friends for drinks at the local bar and grill.

OPERATIONAL STRUCTURE

If you think you can weather the organizational requirements, then you have to worry about operational rules for REITs. Remember, a vast number of big real estate organizations prefer not to be publicly traded because the regulations are numerous and very precise. The basics of the organization of a REIT are as follows:

- Annually, at least 75 percent of the REIT's gross income must be from real estate–related income such as rents from real property and interest on obligations secured by mortgages on real property.

- In addition, 95 percent of the REIT's gross income must be from the prior listed sources, but also can include other passive forms of income such as dividends and interest from non–real estate sources.

- A REIT can own up to 100 percent of the stock of a "taxable REIT subsidiary," a corporation with which a REIT makes a joint election that can earn such income.

- Quarterly, at least 75 percent of a REIT's assets must consist of real estate assets such as real property or loans secured by real property.[11]

The modern REIT era was said to begin with the 1991 IPO of Kimco Realty Corp., a New Hyde Park, New York–based owner and manager of neighborhood and community shopping centers. However, others might argue the modern REIT era didn't begin until one year later, when Taubman Centers Inc., a Bloomfield Hills, Michigan, owner and operator of shopping malls, went public as the country's first umbrella partnership REIT, or UPREIT.

SOLVING A TAX PROBLEM

It's hard to separate real estate investing from tax consequences, and the UPREIT addressed an important point in the transfer (sale) of real estate to the corporate structure of the REIT: The proceeds of that sale were taxed.

The UPREIT creates a tiered ownership encompassing a realty operating partnership (OP) and a REIT, which is the general partner of the OP.

In essence, this is what happens: Property owners who want to divest their properties can contribute those prized investments to the OP in exchange for ownership interests in the OP on a tax-deferred basis (IRC Section 721). This interest is convertible after a period of time into cash or shares of the REIT.[12] (Without confusing the matter, there is something called a 721 UPREIT whereby properties can be transferred into the structure of 1031 tenant-in-common program.)

In the common UPREIT, the partners in an existing real estate partnership and in the REIT become partners in a new partnership,

MEET THE MAVERICK FINANCIERS

Alfred Taubman

Birth Date: 1924

Occupation: Founder, The Taubman Centers

Education: Attended University of Michigan, Lawrence Technological University

Career Highlights:

- Created superregional mall
- Created and codified mall features such as ring road, food court, and dual-level entrances
- Designed malls with improved traffic circulation
- Owned a portfolio of department stores
- Chairman of Sotheby's, the art auction company

the OP. In exchange for the property interests, the real estate owners receive units in the OP. The great part of all this is that this transaction does not result in a taxable transaction—taxes are actually deferred.

Under general circumstances, the taxes remain deferred as long as the UPREIT holds the property and the seller holds the OP units. The seller gets the deferment until such time as the seller decides to dispose of the OP units or converts them into shares of the REIT. Typically, the OP units are exchangeable on a one-for-one basis into REIT common shares.[13]

The great ancillary benefit of the UPREIT structure is that when your REIT wants to expand by buying a property or portfolio of properties, that owner may balk once the tax consequences of the sale are considered. If a sale is arranged and instead of cash the owner receives OP units in the acquiring company, then the tax consequences are deferred.

Humphrey Hospitality Trust Inc., a Norfolk, Nebraska–based owner of nationally franchised, limited-service hotels in secondary and tertiary markets, often promotes itself to owners of those hotels as having the UPREIT advantage.

"Our UPREIT structure," the company proffers, "provides a significant, competitive advantage in the acquisition of additional lodging properties. Property owners can sell their limited-service hotels for UPREIT units, which are the one-for-one equivalent of a share of common stock."[14]

In the transaction, Humphrey Hospitality adds, the seller exchanges the cash flow from one property for the cash flow from a significant portfolio of hotels—the benefits being diversified risk and a more stable, predictable stream of income.[15]

THE TALE OF TAUBMAN CENTERS

The irony about the UPREIT is that the company that started it all, Taubman Centers Inc., has never been an aggregator of big portfolios. As a shopping mall owner and operator, its stable of properties remains relatively small, around 20 properties.

For three generations, the Taubmans have been involved in real estate. About the middle of the last century, Philip Taubman left the automobile industry to start a construction company, mostly building single-family homes and small retail buildings. After World War II, his son Alfred (A. Alfred Taubman) started his own business, borrowing $5,000. The son was much more aggressive and visionary than the father, who joined his son in the new business.

The company was based in Pontiac, a suburb of Detroit; Motor City was then at its apogee. The city's population was nearly 2 million; jobs in the auto industry were plentiful, as American car companies ruled the world; and along with the burgeoning middle class, the suburbs expanded wildly.

In 1955, Alfred Taubman developed his first shopping center in Flint, Michigan, but his big break came a year later when Max Fisher, a local entrepreneur who owned an oil refinery, bought up a chain of small discount gas stations called Speedway 79. Fisher hired Taubman's company to upgrade the old stations and build new ones. In a three-year period, Taubman assiduously did just that, constructing or remodeling more than 150 stations.

In 1961, Taubman opened his first enclosed shopping center in Ann Arbor, Michigan. It was in this niche that Alfred's vision and talent blossomed. Among his many accomplishments in the advancement of mall design and operations, Alfred Taubman continually pushed the envelope in size, creating what at the time were the largest malls in the country. His Woodfield Mall in Schaumburg, Illinois, at 2 million square feet, is considered the first superregional shopping mall in the United States.

He also codified the food court as a shopping mall staple, enhanced floor design, elevated the concept of sight lines within the mall, created the first "ring road" (the perimeter road that circles many large malls), and pioneered dual-level parking, with access into the mall on two different floors, which helped traffic circulate on all floors of the mall.

During the go-go years of the early 1980s, when real estate development expanded exponentially, The Taubman Company, along with a few other shopping mall companies, expanded by buying department stores, the anchors of many of their developments.

In 1984, the company acquired Woodward & Lothrop in Washington, D.C., and then, in 1986, John Wanamaker in Philadelphia.

Like its other forays into the department store world, these investments would prove disastrous.

Actually, as early as the late 1970s, Taubman began a series of investments outside of malls. The first was in the Irvine Ranch of Orange County, California, which proved a bonanza—Taubman netted $150 million in profit.[16] The second, which looked good at first but proved calamitous, was his 1983 investment in Sotheby's, the art auction company. While it seemed as though Taubman had done an excellent job as chairman in organizing what was then a chaotic organization, he had also engaged in some financial shenanigans and was convicted of price fixing. He was later sentenced to one year in prison.

By the late 1970s, A. Alfred Taubman also began delegating more of the operations of the Taubman Centers to others. After a couple of strong presidents, the mantle passed to Robert Taubman, A. Alfred Taubman's oldest son, who in 1987 became chief operating officer, then president and chief executive officer in 1990. It was under the aegis of Robert Taubman that the Taubman Centers broke new ground in the creation of REITs. In 1992, the company became the first to go public under the structure of an umbrella partnership—the UPREIT.

Taubman Centers corporate office sits in a nondescript office building in the leafy suburban Detroit town of Bloomfield Hills. The building is just not as glamorous as some of the Taubman Centers malls, such as the Mall at Millenia in Orlando; the Mall at Short Hills in Short Hills, New Jersey; or Beverly Center in Los Angeles.

Here's a taste of the good life as defined by a Taubman Centers shopping experience. The Mall at Millenia features Neiman Marcus, Bloomingdale's, Hugo Boss, Jimmy Choo, Louis Vuitton, Tiffany, Cartier, and Chanel.

Over at the Waterside Shops at Pelican Bay, where Taubman is a partner in the development (the company purchased a joint-venture interest in December 2003), it recently added Hermes, Burberry, Gucci, Tiffany, and Christofle. Meanwhile, a Saks Fifth Avenue opened at Willow Bend (Plano, Texas), putting the center in an exclusive group of only 13 other properties in the nation with the anchor combination of Saks and Neiman Marcus.

THE SON ALSO RISES

Robert Taubman is not as imposing as his father was in his prime, a tall, well-dressed man who effused drive and ambition. But he is just as ambitious, just as strong a manager, and boasts a calculator mind just right for the earnings-driven REIT industry, as opposed to the entrepreneur-developer model so typical of his father's era.

You can say what you want about nepotism, but Robert Taubman, now chairman, president, and chief executive, was the right Taubman—the right man—to bring the company into the modern REIT era.

One might say Robert Taubman grew up in shopping centers.

"My brother Bill and I used to take our picnics in shopping centers and construction sites," Taubman recalls. "My father used to have these leasing logs that had different colors for every shopping center. He read them before going to sleep at night, but we would take them out of his briefcase and read them as well."

While at Boston University, where Taubman received his bachelor's degree in economics, he used to skip class and go to one of his dad's Connecticut developments to help lease space. Leasing was something Taubman excelled at. As one longtime Taubman executive told me, "He was an absolute killer leasing agent. Bobby [Robert Taubman] was a legendary leasing agent."

From 1976 to 1979, Taubman worked as a leasing agent in Washington, D.C., then left the family company to worked on the West

Coast. In 1982, he moved back to Taubman headquarters as senior vice president; five years later he moved up to chief operating officer; then in 1991 he became president and chief executive officer.

When I met Taubman in the company's small conference room, he had just flown in from a long trip and was functioning on only three hours of sleep. I didn't quite notice his weariness, as he was all adrenalin, and when it came time to explain the originations of the UPREIT, he went to a whiteboard and mapped out the long string of financial relationships that make up the REIT. What were meaningful diagrams to him looked like a muddle to me, but I certainly wasn't going to tell him that—especially when he was so involved in his explanations.

CREATING LIQUIDITY

The reason the company went public, Taubman explains, was that it was looking for a way to consolidate business, create a singular balance sheet, create liquidity for some of the investors (including longtime investor General Motors pension system), build a company where employees would have a greater sense of ownership, and, perhaps most important, unlock the tax conundrum of real estate ownership.

"They used to say real estate had a high-class problem. Everybody was rich," said Taubman. "They had a high net worth, but no liquidity. They had only cash flow. The only way to have liquidity was to sell an asset, but that would mean a huge tax payment based on the full gain now recaptured from the depreciation."

Here was the problem in a taxing nutshell. If a building cost $100 to build, and you depreciate it $10 a year, and you want to sell it after the fourth year, then your tax basis is $60. However, if the

MEET THE MAVERICK FINANCIERS

Robert Taubman

Birth Date: 1953

Occupation: Chairman, Chief Executive and President of Taubman Centers Inc.

Education: BA, economics, Boston University

Career Highlights:

- Taubman Centers became first UPREIT to go public
- Reduced ownership of Taubman Centers by outside investor
- Beat back hostile takeover attempt from Simon Property Group
- Increased investor returns

structure is now worth $150, then it's a $90 gain based on the tax basis of $60—the capital gains tax would be on the $90.

Actually, not everyone was rich. The close of the 1980s and beginning of the 1990s was marked by a devastating real estate recession, and a lot of big real estate owners (including Donald Trump, Sam Zell, and Paul Reichmann of Olympia & York) were in serious trouble. The Taubman centers weren't in such dire straits, but they did need to recapitalize.

The *Wall Street Journal* tidily summed up the situation this way: "Desperate for cash after an industrywide real estate collapse in the 1990s, dozens of new REITs sought to go public. But to avoid triggering huge capital gains taxes on the real estate owned by the developers, the industry invented a two-tiered structure, known as the UPREIT, that left properties in the hands of an operating partnership, in which power is shared by founders and the newly public REIT."[17]

The UPREIT also solved the problem of consolidating individual partnerships. For large developments, whether shopping malls or high-rise office buildings, many of the deals were done as specific partnerships. If you developed five large projects over five years, that could mean five different partnerships, either with the same or different capital sources.

The Taubman Company actually had been inching toward the UPREIT since 1985, when it created the first pool of partnership interests. "No one had ever taken one partnership interest and another partnership interest and put them together into one pool," says Taubman. "But we took 15 of our shopping centers, put them together into one pool, and against it the GM pension system lent us $650 million."

MULTITIERED OWNERSHIP

That worked financially, but it created a weird operating structure. "While they were not an owner, they were just a lender, but they had an option to become an owner," Taubman explains. "If we wanted to renovate a property and we were going to put $20 million into that property, in essence we were putting in capital as 100 percent owner, though we could end up as only 50 percent owner. We were improving the lender's position, yet not getting a return based on our full investment."

When Taubman went public as an UPREIT, it owned 19 centers. That grew to 25 in 1998, when the ownership changed. The split in ownership at the time of the IPO looked like this: 26 percent of the partnership units in the hands of the Taubmans, 41.5 percent percent in the hands of GM, and the remaining 32.5 percent owned by UPREIT (the public ownership). In addition, GM owned 6 percent of the REIT directly.

By 1998, because it was a pension fund and made the loans to Taubman as an investment, GM didn't want to be in a position of management, so the two entities made an exchange. The operator partnership traded the ownership of 10 shopping centers to GM (kept the management) for partnership units (50 million units). Since the REIT already had 53 million units of the resulting total of 84 million units, it controlled the partnership that owned the 15 properties. Still, it managed all 25 at the time of the transaction.

The GM pension system cashed out.

To understand what this all meant in the end, I poked through an annual report. Ownership—and the report used this phrasing—"at the time of the company's initial public offering and acquisition of its partnership interest," which sounds curious until one reads further and clarification appears: Taubman Centers Inc. (the REIT) owns a managing general partnership interest in the The Taubman Realty Group Limited Partnership, through which it conducts all operations. The operating partnership owns, develops, acquires, and operates regional shopping centers nationally.[18]

Oddly enough, all these arcane points of ownership, including voting rights that go along with ownership, rose to importance in 2003 when Taubman Centers fended off a hostile $1.68 billion takeover attempt by rival shopping center REIT, Simon Property Group Inc.

Apparently, another benefit to going public is flexibility of share issuance. When Taubman Centers restructured in 1998, the REIT issued a new class of stock, Series B, to the Taubman family and a few others in order to move governance from the partnership to the

REIT level. The new structure increased the public's ownership to 63 percent and proportionately gave the Taubmans a 30.6 percent voting block in the REIT (an effective veto, as transactions required support by two-thirds of all voting shares).[19]

But that was all in the future.

CREATING OPPORTUNITIES AND DOLLARS

Back in 1992, it was all about the UPREIT. "This was fundamental," says Taubman. "It created the opportunity for us to go public—and for the rest of the world. If you look at the top 50 REITs, nearly two-thirds are UPREITs. It really unlocked the public capital markets to real estate. And then it allowed big companies to grow the way they have done, including consolidation of the REIT industry."

Prior to The Taubman Centers' IPO, there were 138 publicly listed REITs representing less than $13 billion in market capitalization.[20] Today, almost 200 public REITs command a market capitalization of close to $300 billion. That's an increase of way over 1,000 percent "since we led the way," says Taubman.

Investors willing to take the chance on Taubman back in 1992 wouldn't have done so badly, either.

The company went public with 19 assets and by 2004 had built 10 more plus acquired 6. Out of those 35 shopping malls, it sold 14, including the 10 exchanged with the GM pension system. At the time I visited the Taubmans, the company had 21 centers and 2 more under construction. Not a lot of growth, I said to Robert Taubman.

About the only concern in regard to The Taubman Centers is its small profile. Although Simon Property Group, a serial acquirer, didn't get to take over Taubman Centers, it bought Chelsea Property Group in 2004 and now owns about 300 properties.

The same year, General Growth Properties acquired The Rouse Co. and now has over 200 properties, while the much smaller Macerich Co. nabbed privately held Wilmorite Holdings LP and now owns more than 60 shopping malls.

"In the shopping center business we are the only ones that aren't consolidators. Everybody else is a consolidator," A. Alfred Taubman muses. "We like our business."

Backing up his father's viewpoint to the maximum, the son tossed out some pertinent numbers: "Our funds from operation (FFO) per share has grown from $0.83 to $1.99, so we have achieved a compounded annual growth rate of over 8 percent."

At the end of 2004, the company announced a 5.6 percent increase in its dividend. This was the ninth consecutive year of increases.[21]

For 2004, Taubman could happily report, "our investors enjoyed a 51.7 percent total return, one of the best among REITs. Our total return to shareholders over the 10 years ended December 31, 2004, was 527 percent, or a compound annual growth rate of just over 20 percent. Sales per square foot increased 8.2 percent for the full year, reaching a record level of $477 per square foot."[22]

He concluded, "We have worked hard to create shareholder value."[23]

A TRUE MAVERICK'S APPROACH TO REITS AND UPREITS

1. Any type of real estate portfolio works for a REIT.
2. Since REITs are publicly traded, the stock market gives value to your shares.
3. REITs are a good vehicle for growth.
4. The downside of REITs is that share price can tumble quickly.
5. REITs are subject to stringent regulations.
6. REITs must distribute 90 percent of taxable income to shareholders.
7. At least 75 percent of the REIT's gross income must be from real estate.
8. The UPREIT solves a key tax problem in regard to corporate formations.
9. The UPREIT structure is very useful when buying out investors, who in turn have to worry about tax consequences.
10. The downside to UPREITs is that they have a complex ownership structure.

CHAPTER 12

The REITs That Don't Trade Publicly

Not all real estate investment trusts were created equal. About a decade ago, some bright investment managers decided REITs, a useful and popular real estate entity, didn't have to be traded on a stock exchange, but could be left in private hands to function in ways very similar to a limited partnership.

In my first book, one chapter spotlighted the Houston developer Hines, builder of some of the best-designed high-rise office towers in the Southwest and elsewhere around the world. Gerald Hines founded the firm, but by the time I interviewed him, the company had passed into the capable hands of his son, Jeffrey Hines, who was already moving the firm into a different space in the real estate world.

In 2003, the real estate industry was a bit taken aback when Hines unveiled its new direction; it introduced a public, nontraded real estate investment trust.

Similar to the publicly traded REIT, a nontraded REIT is required to pay dividends to investors of at least 90 percent of its net income. Nontraded REITs are registered with the SEC, but they don't trade on any public exchange.

Hines had some very aggressive intentions, as its registration statement reported it would be raising $2.2 billion. I haven't spoken to Jeffrey Hines since I interviewed him for my first book, but things may have been slower than he expected, because SEC filings report that he raised just $93 million through the first quarter of 2005. When I checked the 2004 annual report of the Hines nontraded REIT, there had already been a quick accumulation of high-rise office properties, although as one source noted, the Hines REIT initially started by buying up the fractional ownership interest of other Hines-owned buildings in the portfolio of other funds.

If there was a heyday, if not a watershed year, for nontraded REITs, it was not so very long ago in the real estate–busy but contentious year of 2003.

In that year, four of the biggest sponsors of nontraded REITs—Wells Real Estate Funds, Inland Group, CNL Financial Group, and W.P. Carey & Co. LLC—doubled their combined total assets from

$11.5 billion to $21.1 billion.[1] No wonder Hines decided to join the party.

Here's another statistic from that year: Retail investors pumped $6 billion of capital into those same big four—roughly half of that amount raised by Norcross, Georgia–based Wells Real Estate Funds Inc.[2] Wells was just getting started. In November 2003, the company launched the behemoth Wells REIT II, a $7.77 billion offering.

NEW INVESTMENT UNVEILED

None of this Wells Real Estate ascendancy was a surprise to Leo F. Wells III, the folksy, God-fearing president of Wells Real Estate Funds, who pioneered the nontraded REIT, having launched his first one in 1998.

Back then, what Wells wanted to do was to relieve the publicly traded REIT of its volatility. "With a publicly traded REIT, someone comes out and says REITs are great, and what happens? The price goes up and the dividend goes down," he says. "Then someone writes an article that says REITs are terrible. Everybody calls their broker and sells. With the publicly traded REIT you get immediate liquidity, but you also get volatility. As a provider of investment products for the financial planning community, I wanted to create a product that would place investors' money into a diversified investment for a 10-year period, where the account is not turning all the time. The nontraded REIT is perfect for that, because investors put their money in and it just stays put. They cannot call up every day and say buy or sell."

Did Wells create the first nontraded REIT? Absolutely not, but he certainly put the investment vehicle on the map. "There may have been some around, but none come to mind," he says today. "If there were, they weren't focused on the long-term lease aspect of office and industrial properties. What our investors really wanted was dependable cash flow."

COMPARISONS ARE IN ORDER

As with publicly traded REITs, the nontraded REITs are corporations with pools of money raised for real estate investment purposes. By and large, the similarities end there. The National Association of Real Estate Investment Trusts breaks the nontraded REITs into two categories, "private REITs" and "non-exchange-traded REITs," and then compares them both to publicly traded REITs.

- *Overview.* Public REITs file with the SEC and shares trade on a national stock exchange. Non-exchange-traded REITs file with the SEC, but shares do not trade on exchanges. Private REITs do not register with the SEC and shares do not trade.

- *Liquidity.* Public REITs have minimum liquidity standards. Non-exchange-traded REITs have limited redemption programs and minimum holding periods, and investors' exit strategy is linked to required liquidation period (10 years) or listing of stock on exchange. Private REITs' redemption programs vary by company and are generally limited in nature.

- *Transaction costs.* For public REITs, broker commissions typically run between $20 and $150 per trade, and investment banks receive a 2 to 7 percent underwriting fee. For non-exchange-traded REITs, 10 to 15 percent (9.5 percent for Wells) of gross offering proceeds go to pay broker-dealer commissions; offering expenses and advisory fees split between related intermediary and third-party broker-dealer. For private REITs, costs vary by company.

- *Management.* Public REITs are self-advised and self-managed. Non-exchange-traded REITS are externally advised and managed. Private REITs are externally advised and managed.

- *Minimum investment amount.* For public REITs, it's one share. For non-exchange-traded REITs, it's typically $1,000 to $2,500. For private REITs, it's typically $1,000 to $2,500 (those designed for institutional investors require a much higher minimum).[3]

In some regards the nontraded REIT mostly looks like the old real estate limited partnership, except that REITs have an independent board of directors. Both are investment vehicles that own diversified portfolios of real estate and pay out most of their rental income in the form of dividends. Both issue shares. The appraisal value, unlike with a publicly traded REIT, is the share price. Both are designed to deliver income and appreciation. Early in the new millennium, yields from both were in the 6 to 8 percent range, which was very attractive when Treasury bills were yielding 1.6 percent. And both have high commission fees. In regard to the latter, using W.P. Carey & Co.'s limited partnerships as an example, commissions and acquisition costs run to 13 percent. Meanwhile, Wells nontraded REITs charge 9.5 percent overall (7 percent to the financial representative, 1.5 percent to the broker-dealer, and 1 percent to Wells Investment Securities)—provided one ponies up the minimum $1,000 investment (fees drop to 3 percent for those who invest over $1 million), plus there is an additional charge of 2 percent of each dollar raised to cover acquisition costs involved in buying properties.[4]

NOT WITHOUT CRITICISM

So much of a private REIT's hefty fees go to paying commission to planners, the *Wall Street Journal* reports, that as little as 84 cents per dollar invested goes for the actual real estate. In addition, since most private REITs resort to external advisory arrangements, which have additional fees and costs, a significant portion of money is not invested.[5]

The *Wall Street Journal* wasn't the only business publication to criticize fee bleeding in regard to private REITs. *Forbes* magazine reports that REITs are pretty liberal about the fees being siphoned off for insiders. Using Wells as an example, the magazine asserted that to ensure tenants maintain property, Wells REIT buys that service from Wells Management Co. Inc., to which it pays a fee of 4.5 percent of rent roll (1.5 percent for a triple net lease is standard); Wells Real Estate Funds gets a 2.5 percent cut on the purchase price for advice on which properties to buy; and Wells Investment Securities gets "lush" fees (about 16 percent of all capital garnered) on the raising of new capital.[6]

Among the many Wells-led firms are Wells Management Co. Inc., which can be engaged to manage Wells Real Estate Funds properties; Wells Development Corporation, which develops real estate properties; Wells Asset Management Inc., an investment advisor to the Wells family of real estate funds; and Wells Capital, advisor to Wells Real Estate Funds.

THE JOYS OF PRIVATE REITS

As an investment manager, investor, and organizer of real estate investments, what Leo Wells likes about the nontraded REIT is that he can be specific in terms of the asset class he seeks as investments, and mostly he wants office and industrial properties. "I like the idea of having good, big office and industrial buildings that are net leased [tenants pay all the expenses] for a 10-year period of time," Wells explains. "Because what our investors want is a steady, dependable cash flow, and you are able to get that with these types of properties.

It is not the properties but the tenants that pay rent, and you can get those kinds of tenants with these kinds of properties."

Wells set his sights on fairly big portfolios, with assets totaling $4 billion to $6 billion. The idea is that size brings safety. In other words, if one or two or even three buildings perform badly it won't take down the portfolio and the REIT can continue to pay regular dividends. "For instance, our Wells REIT [Wells Real Estate Investment Trust Inc.] is still at a 7 percent dividend after all of these years in spite of what has happened in the real estate market, mostly because we have these long-term leases," he says.

This doesn't mean that the nontraded REITs can't time the market when necessary. In April 2005, Wells REIT sold 27 office and industrial properties to publicly traded REIT Lexington Corporate Properties Trust for $786 million. According to the company, the 5.1 million square feet of properties were acquired or developed between 1999 and 2003. Most were Class A office buildings with single tenants of investment-grade ratings. At the time, Wells noted, "we viewed the sale as an exercise in effective portfolio management that allows us to fine-tune our investment strategy while capitalizing on today's attractive investment sales market to capture gains for our shareholders."

Those who invest in nontraded REITs enjoy the following advantages:

- The value of nontraded REITs cannot be affected by such outside factors as interest rate change, corporate scandal, and sector developments irrelevant to the value of the assets held.

- Nontraded REITs do not suffer from the market volatility that can adversely impact publicly traded REITs.

- Owners of nontraded REITs are individuals enabled to purchase some of America's finest commercial buildings that previously were available only to high-net-worth individuals or institutions.

• REITS, whether publicly traded or nontraded, provide for a single level of tax on income at the individual level—similar to a partnership, an S corporation, or any other flow-through entity. Also, tax-exempt investors do not incur unrelated business income tax (UBIT) with respect to REIT investments.[7]

INVESTMENT HAPPINESS

For investors, the attractions are numerous. After a set period of time, often 10 years but ranging from 7 to 14 years, nontraded REITs are either taken public or liquidated and the proceeds distributed to investors. Meanwhile, over the course of all those years, investors receive a very handsome dividend, usually in the 7 to 8 percent range. That is a higher dividend than most public REITs offer. In fact, the average dividend yield for a public REIT stood at 5.5 percent. However, not everyone can buy nontraded REITs; minimum net asset threshold for investors is often about $150,000 (excluding one's home) or gross annual income of $45,000. Investors must buy a minimum amount as well—about 250 shares, or $2,500 worth (110 shares at $1,000 at Wells).[8]

The key thing to understand about an investment in a nontraded REIT is that it is not a liquid investment such as a publicly traded REIT. In the latter, you can buy and sell shares at any time. That is not the case with nonpublic REITs.

To exit a nontraded REIT, generally shareholders can redeem their investment only upon the occurrence of a liquidity event: (1) the predetermined date a nontraded REIT liquidates its assets; (2) the nontraded REIT selling or merging with a publicly traded

REIT, or (3) a nontraded REIT listing on a stock exchange and becoming a publicly traded REIT. As an example, Wells REIT was launched in 1998 and closed to investors in 2003. Its predetermined end date is 2008. If shareholders want out before that, they may do so at full share value only if they are among the first 5 percent of all shareholders to request share redemption in a given year—or in the event of death or disability. Otherwise, they must wait until the following year. The process also takes some time because the request for redemption has to go to the board of directors for approval.[9]

MISUNDERSTOOD MARKETING

Perhaps the most controversial aspect of nontraded REITs has to do with how they are marketed to the public. Some people would say they are flogged to prospective investors, but it's not necessary to be so harsh. Suffice it to say they are "heavily marketed," almost exclusively through financial planners and advisors. Unlike publicly traded REITs, they have a fixed price of approximately $10 a share.[10]

The problem for the REIT is the sale process, the first flash point being the commissions. The fee structures are usually set at 10 to 15 percent and go toward the payment of broker-dealer commissions, offering expenses, and up-front acquisition fees. According to a Wells executive, an up-front fee of 9.5 percent is charged to the investor, with 7 percent of that going toward the financial planner who sold the shares. That seems to be a problem for critics of the product, who assert that the commissions compel financial planners to push nontraded REIT shares over other investment alternatives. A *Real Estate Forum* article from 2004 claims that nonpublic REITs are sold because "there are high fees associated with them; it's very lucrative for the financial planning distribution system," and financial planners are "motivated to sell this product at a fairly heavy commission."[11]

To this Wells responds, "Shares of the nontraded REIT can also be purchased on a no-load basis for fee-based planners who charge an annual asset management fee (1 to 2 percent per year). When you consider a commission-based planner is earning his fee up front on a long-hold investment, the investor often comes out ahead."

Another nontraded REIT sponsor, Oak Brook, Illinois–based Inland Real Estate Group of Companies Inc., reveals its Inland Western Retail Real Estate Trust Inc. has a deep reliance on broker-dealers.

Inland Western Retail is registered with the Securities and Exchange Commission, although according to the prospectus its shares are not listed or traded on any exchange. The nonpublic REIT seeks to acquire retail properties primarily west of the Mississippi River. The current portfolio consists of more than 60 properties. It is sold only by broker-dealers authorized to do so. Specifically, the nonpublic REIT is sponsored by Inland Real Estate Investment Corp., which has the specific purpose of developing real estate investment products for the broker-dealer community.

Since nonpublic REIT shares are considered by some to be "sold, not bought," it raises concerns that there is potentially a lot of face-to-face salesmanship. The Wells REIT, for example, is offered through a group of approximately 400 affiliated broker-dealers and thousands of independent reps, whom Wells executives "pump up" at annual conferences.[12]

Unfortunately for Leo Wells, the National Association of Securities Dealers didn't take too kindly toward the lavish self-promotion of these conferences. In 2003, NASD censured Wells Investment and Leo Wells, in particular, fining them a total of $150,000. NASD also suspended Leo Wells from acting in a principal capacity for one year.

According to NASD, conferences held by Wells Investment in 2001 and 2002 that were touted as being "strictly educational" were instead "lavish affairs that did not meet the standards of NASD rules. The meetings included a Friday night sock hop, a beach bash and dinner at a Civil War fort with costumed Civil War heroes, fireworks, fife and drum players, skydivers, and a cannon reenactment," the NASD reported. The representatives' guests were also treated to free food, transportation, lodging, and golf. Wells Investment provided less than 13 hours of training and education during the three full days of each conference. In settling the dispute, Wells neither admitted nor denied the allegations, but said it would abide by NASD rules at future conferences.[13]

NOT SO EASY TO ORGANIZE

Considering the fact that as much as $6 billion a year in investment dollars goes to nontraded REITs, it would seem to be an investment vehicle others would want to emulate. It's not.

When asked about it, Wells, who has a funny, self-deprecating conversational style, laughed. "A lot of people think if Leo Wells can do it, it must be easy because he has no brains at all and went to the University of Georgia. Well, I have had a number of people tell me it took twice as long and cost twice as much as they thought it would to get started. Some have been successful; some haven't raised a lot of money."

A simple, private REIT can be done, although Wells doesn't advise it. "You can do a private REIT by yourself and do it relatively inexpensively, but that would just mean you own a bunch of real estate and want it in a REIT structure."

The important point is that to attract outside investors, diversification is the only way to go. To get optimal diversification you need to spend a lot of money to acquire properties in different geographic locations that are leased to a variety of tenants in diverse industries.

"Most private REITs don't raise enough money to make them work," Wells cautions. "You have to have a lot of diversification, and you cannot wait 40 years to get that. If it takes forever to get diversification, your customer is not advantaged."

As an investor, if you and a bunch of partners already have a portfolio of properties, then a decision has already been made regarding the form of ownership, Wells adds. Generally, it is some sort of limited partnership—and that's okay. The limited partnership protects everyone from liability, and it's cheap to construct. Wells, who obviously thinks big—the necessity of achieving a minimum of $4 billion to $5 billion in investments for his nontraded REITs—maintains the cost of forming a REIT is so high that it is prohibitive for most investment groups.

HUMBLE TO RUMBLE

Probably nobody who operates in the real estate business on a national scale can toss off that good ol' boy shtick like him. Maybe it's his secret weapon? Just when you think you're dealing with some trailer park habitué, he slams shut that deal on you before you even realize there was a transaction on the table. The folksiness hides an amazing real estate mind. Not only did Wells take the real estate formation called the nontraded REIT and create a phenomenon, he also figured out the best way to get this concept across to the public. It was a lot of moving parts, and he got them all facing in the same direction very quickly.

The nontraded REIT had been around since the beginning of the 1990s, but it was used mostly by institutional investors. Wells retooled this corporate structure and brought it to the attention of the American investing public.

Born and raised in rural south Georgia, near the town of Valdosta, Wells went to the University of Georgia, where he majored in economics. He thought about a career in law and did attend law school at night for a year and a half, but as he recalls, "I slept through most of the classes."

Wells's family were mostly farm people, but his parents had branched out, and they operated the first Dairy Queen in the state. As it turned out, that was all the background Wells needed. When he left law school in 1962, he went to work for the southeastern division of International Dairy Queen, traveling about north Georgia inspecting properties.

Dairy Queen was in an expansion mode during the 1960s, and the amiable and energetic Wells quickly moved out of inspection and into selling franchises. It was like putting Thomas Edison in charge of the toolshed. With his gift of gab, Wells immediately became king of the sales pitch. "I sold so many franchises that first year, it was going to take them five years to build all the stores," he laughs. "I essentially worked myself out of a job."

Wells was too good to lose, so Dairy Queen sent him off to help find real estate for all the franchises he sold. Once again, he was too sharp for the position. "I really enjoyed and did well at what I was doing to the extent that some people in the real estate brokerage business convinced me to leave Dairy Queen and try my hand at real estate," he says.

Wells did. Around 1970, he went to work at a local real estate company in Atlanta. That lasted about two years, until Wells decided to set up a separate real estate company, finally getting serious enough to create Wells & Associates in 1974.

At the beginning of the 1970s, real estate was literally a wide-open business, especially in the South. Although he worked for a

MEET THE MAVERICKS

Leo F. Wells III

Birth Date: 1944

Occupation: Founder, President, and Director of Wells Real Estate Funds Inc.; President and Director of Wells REIT; President, Treasurer, and Director of Wells Capital; President of Wells & Associates Ins.; Trustee of Wells Family of Real Estate Funds; and President, Treasurer, and Director of Wells Management Company Inc., Wells Advisors Inc., Wells Development Corporation and Wells Asset Management Inc.

Education: BA, business, University of Georgia

Career Highlights:

- Put together some of the first registered limited partnerships
- Founded Wells Real Estate Funds Inc.
- Created the first mutual fund to track a REIT index
- Pioneered the nontraded REIT concept
- Is one of the largest owners of corporate offices in the United States

brokerage company, Wells was already putting together syndications—just about from the moment he started his real estate career. Not only was he working with individual investors, but also with the trust departments of the local banks, who could invest in real estate and liked his syndications. "I did rather well," Wells recalls. "The investors included several banks that had pension and trust funds, and they ended up doing very well."

He adds, "That's the great thing about making people money. They tell other people."

More important to Wells was that he discovered a business he liked. "I enjoyed the whole process. I enjoyed everything from sitting on someone's front porch, rocking all day as we tried to figure out what to do with their real estate, to helping them figure where to put their money. I enjoyed the involvement of people on both sides of the deal."

REPRESENTING THE MONEY SIDE

Wells was too smart to become fully imbued with the enjoyment of it all. He was already figuring out the industry and was thinking 10 steps ahead of the traditional brokerage company. "Most people in real estate historically represent the property owner. They would find someone who wanted to sell, stick a sign on their property, and wait until someone came around to buy," says Wells. That's not what he wanted to do. He fathomed there was just as good a business representing the money, not the real estate. "People with money would come to me and I would find them the property," he says.

Wells divined the syndication structure. "In the early 1970s, this wasn't a formal process," he explains. "What we did in Atlanta was partnerships. In fact, I did two of the first registered limited partnerships, but all that meant was I found people with money who wanted to invest. Then I found the property. A few years later, I turned around and sold the property. They made money, were happy, and told other people. From that point on, I mainly represented people with money."

The key to working with a group of investors is patience, or as

Wells likes to say, being the sheep dog with a herd of sheep. "You can't move them very fast, but you have to keep them moving in the same direction."

In 1984, Wells established Wells Real Estate Funds, a boutique real estate investment funds company that concentrated mainly on limited partnerships. "I did nothing but limited partnerships until 1997," he says.

That's an amazing record considering what happened to the limited partnership business after the real estate recession of the late 1980s—it almost disappeared.

"We didn't lose any," maintains Wells. "We kept all our properties leased and we didn't have any mortgages because we had paid all cash. The bust caused some problems, such as we might not have been able to keep the buildings full and we couldn't pay out as much cash flow, but we never had to call any investors and ask them to send in more money."

Wells quotes an interesting statistic. In 1984 to 1985, there were 150 real estate sponsors selling limited partnerships at the IAFP convention. Wells Real Estate Funds is the only one of that group still selling today.

To this day, Wells touts the partnership. "It is a great way to own real estate. You limit your liability, and because of the way depreciation is handled it is still a form of tax shelter."

INNOVATIVE CONCEPTS

Not only did Wells maintain a steady business in real estate limited partnerships, but he continued to innovate. In the mid-1990s, he pioneered the first mutual fund to track a REIT index, convincing Standard & Poor's to develop such an index and working with S&P for a year to set it up.[14]

Today, the Wells S&P REIT Index Fund is the only mutual fund available directly to the public that tracks the S&P REIT Composite Index. It provides the highest correlation to the entire securitized real estate market in the United States.

He finally got the mutual fund trading at about the same time he unveiled his first nontraded REIT, which is called Wells REIT.

This took a whole lot of intuition. Despite a roaring comeback in the mid-1990s, REITs still had somewhat of a checkered past, mostly due to the category called mortgage REITs, which went bust in the 1970s. "Mortgage REITs loaned people a lot of money, and when the value of the real estate dropped, they were not able to recover," says Wells. "People lost a lot of money in mortgage REITs."

Nevertheless, the more Wells looked at the structure of the REIT, the more he liked it. Two things really stuck out. First, when people invest in a REIT, they use a Form 1099, not a Schedule K-1 (for partnerships). "There's something psychological about a 1099; people are comfortable with it," says Wells.

Second, REITs have a unique tax structure that is different from a partnership. REITs pay no corporate taxes, which means they have more dividends to pass through to an investor, as the law requires the REIT pay out 90 percent of what is the equivalent of net operating income.

As noted, Wells also doesn't like volatility. Using his own mutual fund as an example, Wells comments, there are some years when it takes in several hundred million dollars and some years when several hundred million goes out the door. "They are getting a dividend, but that is not a long-term goal," says Wells. "Our long-term goal is to get people in real estate for a long enough time so they can really make some money. You want to keep them in for a longer period of time in nontraded investments (such as the nontraded REIT). If you read the data, you find out that investors tend to stay in an investment less than 18 months, which is why most of them never make any money."

Once in a nontraded REIT, such as Wells REIT II, it is not convenient to exit. First, the true exit strategy doesn't happen until October 2015. If Wells REIT II has not listed its shares by then on a national securities exchange or Nasdaq National Market, the board of directors will request stockholders to approve an extension of the listing deadline or a liquidation of the portfolio.

However, if as an investor you want to get out early, there are limited redemption options. First, within two years of death or qualifying disability, shares may be redeemed at $10 per share—the original price. Second, after holding shares for one year, investors may apply to redeem their shares at $9.10 per share. This price is fixed for at least three years after the offering. Thereafter, the redemption price will equal 95 percent of the appraised share value.

The Wells REIT (think of it as Wells REIT I) was created in 1998 and focused on acquiring properties that were leased long term to corporate clients with excellent credit ratings. This provided a steady income stream, enabling Wells to pay an attractive dividend. In 2002, Wells Real Estate Funds was the number one buyer of Class A office properties in the United States.[15] Also, it was the number one buyer of all commercial property in 2003, according to Real Capital Analytics.

That REIT is no longer open to investment and has been supplanted by Wells REIT II.

Initially, the overriding idea was to offer Wells customers investment options. For the first decade of Wells Real Estate Funds, it offered only limited partnerships. The nontraded REIT gave investors a choice.

"We were fortunate in that we already had a good relationship with financial planners and broker-dealers all over the United States with our limited partnerships," says Wells. "So when we came along with this product, it was kind of like going out with two guns instead of one. The financial planners could put their customers in our nontraded REIT, or they could put them in our partnerships. It gave the planner options, which they liked, and they started using the product."

Today, Wells Real Estate Funds offers a variety of investment options: Wells REIT II, Wells S&P REIT Index Fund, Wells Limited Partnerships (as of midyear 2005, no LPs are open to new investment), Wells Money Market Fund, a 1031 exchange program, and Wells Mid-Horizon Value-Added Fund.

Wells himself views his company as an umbrella type organization, but the limited partnerships, well, they receive the "silo" metaphor. Getting folksy, Wells notes, "It's almost like having five or six or seven silos as opposed to having a big barn and everything inside the barn." Actually, there have been 14 limited partnerships, and all are now closed to new investors.

In 2003, Ernst & Young, the big accounting and consulting firm, named Leo Wells as its entrepreneur of the year in the financial services category, noting over the years from 2000 to 2003, in the midst of a stock market slump, clients continually increased investments in Wells Real Estate Funds products. In fact, during the high-tech bust years of 2000 through 2002, annual sales increased almost eightfold.

From 1984 through mid-2005, more than 190,000 individuals across the country have invested (through their financial representatives) in Wells-sponsored investment programs. Collectively, those same programs own more than $6.52 billion in assets representing more than 30 million square feet.

A DIFFERENT CORPORATE CULTURE

When Ernst & Young made its award to Wells, it stated Wells Real Estate Funds had been very successful at earning and keeping investors' trust. A large part of Wells's success rests on the way he manages the organization. Wells employs a team of credit analysts who check the quality of the prospective tenant before they examine the property itself. On the other end, Wells created in 1999 an innovative program called Wells University to educate its force of financial planners and broker-dealers who sell the company's investment products. As part of that program, groups of financial planners spend a day at company headquarters learning about products, as Wells Real Estate Funds likes to ensure that its sales force provides the right service.[16]

The Wells Real Estate Funds corporate culture is about as faith-based as it can get without becoming a religious organization. The closest corporate culture to compare it to would be another Georgia success story, Chick-fil-A Inc., founded by devout Baptist S. Truett Cathy. The Wells Real Estate Funds company creed is "to glorify God and care for people."

At the Wells Real Estate Funds corporate offices, don't expect to hear profanity, dirty jokes, or even to see people in Friday dress-down mode. "We never do a casual program," says Wells.

While the working environment may be strict, there are other benefits. Once a year, the company closes down the offices for three or four days and rents the Ritz Carlton in Amelia Island, Florida, for all of its employees and spouses.

Wells tells me this story. "I was down there at the Ritz Carlton talking to the general manager, and he says to me, 'I want you to know that our employees look forward to your visit. Our maids say you all treat them so nicely and with such respect, and they don't get that treatment from groups normally coming through here.' "

A TRUE MAVERICK'S APPROACH TO PRIVATE REITS

1. Nontraded REITs aim to reduce investment volatility.
2. A nontraded REIT may register with the SEC, but it doesn't trade.
3. Redemption policies are very limited.
4. High costs and fee bleeds can be hurdles to investors, but they are income sources to sponsors.
5. Nontraded REITs have some similarity to limited partnerships.
6. Investment minimums are relatively steep.
7. Big portfolios afford some downside protection.
8. Nontraded REITs toss off a handsome dividend.
9. They are marketed mostly through financial consultants and broker-dealers.
10. Unlike public REITs, nontraded REITS have a fixed price.
11. An end date for the investment is always set.
12. Nontraded REITs are a favorite of long-term investors.

Notes

Chapter 1

1. Suzanne Woolley, Kathleen Morris, Richard Melcher, and Stephanie Anderson Forest, "The New World of Real Estate," *Business Week*, September 22, 1997.
2. "Maquiladora Impact on Yuma," www.gypa.org.
3. "Crowder Files for Chapter 11 in Bankruptcy Organization," *Lubbock Avalanche-Journal*, April 7, 1997.
4. Diane Velasco, "Who's Who in Border Investor Verde Group," *Albuquerque Journal*, March 22, 2004.
5. George Chamberlin, "Investing in Master Limited Partnership Interests," www.financeware.com, February 4, 2004.
6. Diane Velasco, "Who's Who in Border Investor Verde Group," *Albuquerque Journal*, March 22, 2004.
7. Ray Smith, "Failed REIT's Story Offers Some Lessons," *Wall Street Journal*, January 2, 2002.
8. Sophia Oh, "Wielansky Finds Leverage in Regency's Acquisition," *St. Louis Business Journal*, October 23, 1998.
9. "Letter to Shareholders of Security Capital Group," www.securitycapital.com.
10. "Security Capital Buying Out Storage USA," *SNL Real Estate Securities Weekly*, November 12, 2001.

Chapter 2

1. "Real Estate Developing—Loan to Cost and Loan to Value in a Real Estate Construction Loan, www.loanuniverse.com.
2. Ibid.

3. "Real Estate Construction Loans," www.mortgage-expo.com.

4. "SBA Look-Alike," www.kaufmanfinancial.net.

5. "Real Estate Construction Loans," www.mortgage-expo.com.

6. "Commercial Property Types," www.allbex.com.

7. "Bridge Loans Are a Perfect Solution," www.fastcommercialmortgages.com.

8. "Mountain Funding Closes on $23M Bridge Loan," *Charlotte Business Journal,* May 9, 2005.

9. Alex Sturm, "What Is a Bridge Mortgage Loan," http://commercialmortgages .articleinsider.com.

10. "What Is Bridge Financing," www.buyincomeproperties.com, April 25, 2005.

11. "Why Borrowers Need Private Money Loans," www.fastcommercialmortgages .com.

12. "Hard Money Loans from $1 Million," www.lsg1.com.

13. "Permanent Financing," www.cmlv.net.

14. "Financing Investment Properties," www.advancedfundingsolutionsllc.com.

15. "CIBC Closed $18M Loan," *Commercial Property News,* April 1, 2005.

16. "Roberts Realty Investors Inc. Refinances Addison Place Apartments," http://biz .yahoo.com, April 25, 2005.

17. "Pacific Security Capital Secures $8,850,000 of Permanent Financing for a Retail Property in Georgia," www.pacificsecuritycapital.com, November 11, 2004.

18. Alex Sturm, "Understanding a Commercial Real Estate Loan," http://commercial– mortgages.articleinsider.com.

19. Jake Little and Shervin Gabayan, "Low Cost Leverage," *National Real Estate Investor,* February 1, 2004.

20. Ibid.

21. William McInerney and Melissa Hough Hinkle, "Use of Mezzanine Debt in Commercial Mortgage Loans," *New York Law Journal,* September 20, 2004.

22. Michelle Napoli, "Cohens Beat 5-Year Goals for Growth, Diversification," *Commercial Property News,* February 1, 2001.

23. John Salustri, "UpClose: Bruce Cohen of Cohen Financial," www.globest.com, June 17, 2004.

24. Marshall Taylor, "A Commercial Success," *Mortgage Banking,* February 2004.

Chapter 3

1. Mike Fickes, "Meet Fannie and Freddie," *National Real Estate Investor,* June 2001.

2. C. Leslie Banas, "HUD and Fannie Mae Requirements for Borrower Entities," *Michigan Real Property Review,* Winter 2000.

3. Ibid.
4. Fickes, "Meet Fannie and Freddie."
5. "Multifamily—Fannie Mae DUS Program Delegated Underwriting and Servicing (DUS)," www.vermilionmortgage.com.
6. "Red Provides $11.5 Million Fannie Mae DUS Loan for Seniors High-Rise Property in Chicago," www.redcapitalgroup.com, May 19, 2005.
7. "APF Completes Largest Fannie Mae DUS Loan Ever," *Multi-Housing News,* June 2, 2004.
8. "Information Statement," www.freddiemac.com, March 31, 2000.
9. Fickes, "Meet Fannie and Freddie."
10. Ibid.
11. "Fannie Mae DUS MBSs," www.allegiancecapital.com.
12. "Information Statement."
13. "Freddie Mac Loans," www.stanmor.com.
14. "Johnson Capital Provided $4,960,000 for Desert View Apartments in Mesa, Arizona," www.johnsoncapital.com.
15. "Statement of Linda Cheatham, Senior Vice President Berkshire Mortgage Finance, on FHA Multifamily Loan Limit Adjustment Act of 2003," www.financialservices.house.gov.
16. Ibid.
17. Banas, "HUD and Fannie Mae Requirements for Borrower Entities."
18. "542(c) FHA-Insured Multifamily Loan Program," www.nmmfa.org.
19. FHA Section 223(f) Immediate Funding Program," www.arcscommercial.com.
20. "Red Mortgage Capital Provides FHA Financing for Assisted Living Facility," www.redcapitalgroup.com, May 20, 2005.

Chapter 4

1. "Equity Financing," www.pacificsecuritycapital.com.
2. "Preferred Equity Investment Program," www.imrei.com.
3. David Ross, "Mezzanine & Equity Financing to Optimize Your Capital Structure," www.c-lender.com.
4. Ibid.
5. "Equity Financing for Those Caught in the Middle," www.hanoverfinancial.com.
6. Stephen Ursery, "Multifamily Beat," *National Real Estate Investor,* January 1, 2000.
7. "Press Releases," www.franklincapitalgroup.com.

8. "Sonnenblick-Eichner Company Arranges Financing for $130 million Caribbean Resort," www.hotelonline.com.

9. David Ross, "Mezzanine & Equity Financing to Optimize Your Capital Structure," www.c-lender.com.

10. Ibid.

11. "Equity Financing," www.pacificsecuritycapital.com.

12. "Firsts, Seconds, Mezzanine Equity," www.scotmor.ca/products.htm.

Chapter 5

1. Queena Sook Kim, "Storied FAO Is Casualty of Tough Holiday Toy-Pricing War," *Wall Street Journal,* December 3, 2003.

2. Gregory Zuckerman and Ellen Byron, "Big Investors Too Sold on Retail," *Wall Street Journal,* April 14, 2005.

3. Robert Berner, "The Next Warren Buffett?" *Business Week,* November 22, 2004.

4. "Zayre," www.wikipedia.org.

5. Ray Smith, "A Retailer's New Plot," *Wall Street Journal,* April 27, 2005.

6. Ibid.

7. Sue Goff and Joseph Pereira, "Discounter Ames Will Liquidate Inventory, Close All Stores," www.freerepublic.com, August 14, 2002.

8. "Shaw's to Assume 18 Ames Leases," www.icsc.org.

9. Berner, "The Next Warren Buffett?"

10. Ibid.

11. "Alexander's Inc.: Overview," www.hoovers.com.

12. Tom Hals, "A Year Later: Strawbridge Is Gone, Stock's Not," *Philadelphia Business Journal,* March 7, 1997.

13. Joel Groover, "Venture Acquires Rights to Ward Properties," *Retail Traffic,* April 1, 2001.

14. Steve Bergsman, "Uncle Milton," *Real Estate Portfolio,* November/December 2004.

15. Edvard Jorgensen, "Company Spotlight," www.seahorseadvisors.com.

16. Ibid.

17. Ibid.

18. Bergsman, "Uncle Milton."

19. Ibid.

20. "Dear Fellow Shareholders, Partners and Associates," *Kimco Realty Corporation 2004 Annual Report.*

21. Bergsman, "Uncle Milton."

Chapter 6

1. Thomas Kostigen, "Real Estate Limited Partnerships Make Comeback," *Investor's Business Daily,* April 9, 2004.
2. Gregory Taggart, "This Little Piggy," *Wealth Manager,* September 2003.
3. Daniel DiTieri, "Investing in a Real Estate Syndicate," *Real Estate Monitor,* Summer 2003.
4. "Real Estate Syndications," www.arches.uga.edu.
5. Ibid.
6. "Real Estate Syndication," www.dearborn.com.
7. Ibid.
8. Ibid.
9. Ibid.
10. Daniel DiTieri, "Investing in a Real Estate Syndicate."
11. Keith Waggoner, "Real Estate: A Good Alternative to Stocks," *Dallas Business Journal,* January 24, 2003.
12. Toddi Gutner, "Back from the Dead: Limited Partnerships," *Business Week,* July 8, 1996.
13. Daniel DiTieri, "Investing in a Real Estate Syndicate."
14. Thomas Kostigen, "Real Estate Limited Partnerships Make Comeback."
15. "Indirect Ownership: Partnerships," www.pgdc.com.
16. Dan Fitzpatrick, "Urban Retail Properties Has Debt but Still a Viable Real Estate Player," *Pittsburgh Post-Gazette,* February 14, 2000.
17. Neil Weilheimer, "Heitman Pays $120M for Portfolio in Slovakia," *Commercial Property News,* October 6, 2004.
18. Suzann D. Silverman, "Heitman Closes Joint Venture Fund at $400 M," *Commercial Property News,* January 16, 2005.

Chapter 7

1. Christopher Ostrowski, "The REIT Wars," *Real Estate Forum,* May 2004.
2. Parke Chapman, "Unlisted REITs Flush with Capital," *National Real Estate Investor,* January 2004.
3. "Characteristics of Publicly Traded REITs, No-Exchange Traded REITs and Private REITs," www.nariet.com.
4. Lewis Braham, "Sick of Being at the Market's Mercy?" *Business Week,* September 16, 2002.
5. Ostrowski, "The REIT Wars."

6. Stephanie Fitch, "Blind Faith," *Forbes,* September 2003.

7. Stephen Renna, "Roundtable Comment Letter to Joint Committee on Taxation on Tax Law Requirements for Ownership of Private REITs," www.rer.org, August 21, 2003.

8. Ray Smith, "Private REITs Bloom Amid Property Boom," *Wall Street Journal,* February 20, 2004.

9. Ostrowski, "The REIT Wars."

10. Ray Smith, "Private REITs Bloom Amid Property Boom."

11. Ostrowski, "The REIT Wars."

12. Fitch, "Blind Faith."

13. "NASD Fines Wells Over Lavish Trips," *Associated Press,* October 13, 2003.

14. "Leo Wells III of Wells Real Estate Funds Named Ernst & Young Entrepreneur of the Year Winner," www.ey.com.

15. Ibid.

16. Ibid.

Chapter 8

1. William Hart, "Debt Restructuring Problems in the Workout of Troubled Real Estate Assets," www.titlelawnnotated.com.

2. "Towards Greater Transparency in Real Estate Private Equity Funds," www .upenn.edu/researchatpenn/article.php, July 31, 2002.

3. "Kennedy-Wilson Buys Japanese Assets with Colony Capital," www.irei.com, September 18, 1998.

4. Andrew Gomes, "Acquiring Property by Buying Distressed Loans Gains Popularity," *Pacific Business News,* August 28, 1998.

5. Mark Heshmeyer, "Bascom Launches $250M Opportunity Fund," www.costar .com/NewsPublic, August 8, 2003.

6. James Mackintosh, "Bad Loans More Than Double At GMAC," *Financial Times,* March 29, 2005.

7. Form 10KSB, First Community Bank Corp of America, March 22, 2004.

8. "Opportunities for Sellers," www.usacapitalloans.com.

9. "Citigroup Alternative Investments: Distressed Debt," www.smithbarney.com.

10. "Executive Summary for Camelback Capital Corporation," www.camelbackcapital .net.

11. Ibid.

12. Thomas J. Barrack Jr., "Mirror, Mirror on the Wall, Who's the Fairest of Them All," *Chairman's Corner,* April 2003.

13. Ibid.
14. Thomas J. Barrack Jr., "The Unlevel Playing Field," *Chairman's Corner,* March 2003.
15. Ibid.
16. Ibid.
17. Ibid.
18. Ibid.
19. Ibid.

Chapter 9

1. Bendix Anderson, "Conduits Fight Hard for Your Business with Bigger, Faster Loans," *Apartment Finance Today,* March–April 2004.
2. Michael Hoover and Tucker S. Knight, "Look For Commercial Real Estate Loans in All the Right Places," *San Antonio Business Journal,* March 18, 2005.
3. "What Is a Conduit Loan," www.c-loans.com.
4. Hoover and Knight, "Look For Commercial Real Estate Loans in All the Right Places."
5. "What Is a Conduit?" www.croninbisson.com, January 2004.
6. Joe Gose, "Lenders Draw Up Plays to Land Big Deals," *National Real Estate Investor,* February 2005.
7. Ibid.
8. Anderson, "Conduits Fight Hard for Your Business with Bigger, Faster Loans."
9. Hoover and Knight, "Look For Commercial Real Estate Loans in All the Right Places."
10. "What Is a Conduit?" www.croninbisson.com.
11. "Small Loan Conduit Program," www.commercialwholesale.com.
12. Tom Conwell, "The Trick to Using Conduit Financing," www.fairbrookcompany.com.
13. "What Is a Conduit?" www.croninbisson.com.
14. Keat Foong, "Expanding Pool of Sources Now Competing For Small Loans," *Multi-Housing News,* March 1, 2005.
15. "Servicing Issues: The Surprise Cost of Conduit Loans," www.mfloan.com, July 1, 2001.
16. "What Is a Conduit Loan," www.c-loans.com.
17. Gene Walden, "Make More with Mortgage-Backed Securities," www.allstarstocks.com.
18. Jonathan Sears, "Substitute Play," www.newmandefeasance.com.

19. Ibid.

20. Neal Gussis and Shawn Hill, "The Conduit Financing Pool: Assessing Risk in CMBS and the Role of the Rating Agency," *Inside Self-Storage,* www .insideselfstorage.com.

21. Steve Bergsman, "CMBS, REITs Travel Down Parallel Paths to Success," *National Real Estate Investor,* April 1997.

22. "Case Study: Confederation Life Insurance Co.," www.erisk.com.

23. Bergsman, "CMBS, REITs Travel Down Parallel Paths to Success."

24. Steve Bergsman, CMBS: Where We Go from Here," *National Real Estate Investor,* May 1999.

Chapter 10

1. "The Investor's Guide to Real Estate Investment Trusts (REITs)," www .money99.com.

2. "BioMed Realty Trust, Inc. Announces Exercise of Over-Allotment Option and Acquisition of Five Properties," www.biomedrealty.com.

3. "BioMed Realty Trust, Inc. Announces Acquisition of Five Properties and Closing of $100 Million Credit Facility," www.biomedrealty.com.

4. "BioMed Realty Trust Reports Fourth Quarter and Year-End Financial Results: Acquisition Program Ahead of Plan," www.biomedrealty.com.

5. "The Revolution: Necessity Is the Mother of Invention," www.property-mag.com.

6. Ibid.

7. Tim Lemke, "First Potomac Up 25% Since Offering," *Washington Times,* February 24, 2004.

8. Ibid.

9. Ibid.

10. Sheila Muto, "Recent REIT Offerings Have Lackluster Returns," www .realestatejournal.com, December 1, 2004.

11. "Forming and Operating a Real Estate Investment Trust," www.investinreits .com.

12. "The §721 Tax Deferred 'UPREIT' Transfer," www.1031exchange-tic.com/721 .htm.

13. Ibid.

14. "Investors Overview," www.humphreyhospitality.com.

15. Ibid.

16. Francis X. Donnelly, "Price-Fixing Conviction Stains Storied Career," *Detroit News,* December 6, 2001.

17. Dean Starkman and Robin Sidel, "Mall Brawl: Bid Marks REIT Turning Point," *Wall Street Journal,* April 28, 2003.
18. "Notes to Consolidated Financial Statements," *Taubman Centers, Inc. 2002 Annual Report.*
19. Starkman and Sidel, "Mall Brawl."
20. "We're Open for Business," *Taubman Centers, Inc. 2002 Annual Report.*
21. "Taubman Centers Announce Fourth Quarter Earnings," www.taubman.com.
22. Ibid.
23. Ibid.

Chapter 11

1. Edward LaPuma, "Sale-Leaseback as a Component of Deal Financing for Venture Capitalists, Private Equity and LBO Investors," www.wpcarey.com, September 1, 2001.
2. Richard Strotman, "Sale/Leaseback: Financing Tool for the '90s," *CPA Journal Online,* April 1991.
3. "Six Advantages of Sale-Leaseback Financing," www.incomo50.com/leaseback.htm.
4. Strotman, "Sale/Leaseback: Financing Tool for the '90s."
5. "SNH Completes $148.2 Million Purchase and Lease Transaction for 31 Communities from Five Star Quality Care Inc," MSN.Money, November 19, 2004.
6. James Frantz, "Net Lease Financing: Retail Corporations Capitalize on Their Real Estate, *Retail Traffic,* June 1, 2000.
7. Ibid.
8. Charles Keenan, "When It's Smarter to Rent," *Institutional Investor,* May 2003.
9. "Leasing Techniques for Acquisition and Financing," 1999 Real Estate Investment Forum, www.highnoi.com.
10. Keenan, "When It's Smarter to Rent."
11. Ibid.
12. Frantz, "Net Lease Financing: Retail Corporations Capitalize on Their Real Estate."
13. "Six Advantages of Sale-Leaseback Financing," www.incomo50.com/leaseback.htm.
14. Frantz, "Net Lease Financing: Retail Corporations Capitalize on Their Real Estate."
15. Ken Miller, "Off-Balance-Sheet Sale-Leasebacks and Synthetic Leases After Enron," *California Real Property Journal,* Fall 2002.

16. Financial Interpretations Number 45 and 46: The Impact on Corporate Real Estate," www.cresapartners.com.

17. "W.P. Carey & Co. Names Gordon F. DuGan Chief Executive Officer, www .wpcarey.com, March 22, 2005.

18. "W.P. Carey and Finland's TietoEnator Complete $95 Million Sale-Leaseback, www.wpcarey.com, July 26, 2004.

Chapter 12

1. "Bank of America Provides $8.6 Million in Financing to Preserve Affordable Housing on Chicago's South Side," www.bankofamerica.com, March 1, 2005.

2. Jeremy Citro, "Low-Income Housing Tax Credits: Helping Meet the Demand for Affordable Rental Housing," www.aarp.org, January 1999.

3. "Resources for Affordable Housing, www.hahro.org.

4. Citro, "Low-Income Housing Tax Credits: Helping Meet the Demand for Affordable Rental Housing."

5. "Low Income Housing Tax Credits: The Most Lucrative Tax Shelter in American History," www.floridacdc.org.

6. "Resources for Affordable Housing, www.hahro.org.

7. Donna Kimura, "Agencies Attempt to Address Development Costs," *Affordable Housing Finance,* December 2004.

8. Ibid.

9. "About the Low Income Housing Tax Credit Program," www.danter.com.

10. Citro, "Low-Income Housing Tax Credits: Helping Meet the Demand for Affordable Rental Housing.

11. "Resources for Affordable Housing, www.hahro.org.

12. "First New Construction in Years, Adding Stock to Low Vacancies," www .relatedcapital.com.

13. "Using the Low-Income Housing Tax Credit Program for Special Needs Housing," www.dhcr.state.ny/ocd/pubs/htm/litc8.htm.

14. "Resources for Affordable Housing, www.hahro.org.

15. "Using the Low-Income Housing Tax Credit Program for Special Needs Housing," www.dhcr.state.ny/ocd/pubs/htm/litc8.htm.

Index